1

2

3

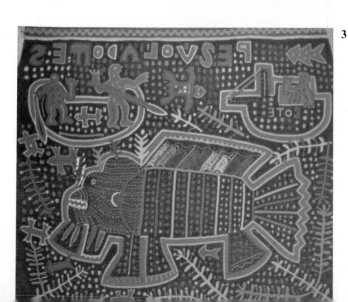

4

5

6

7

8

9

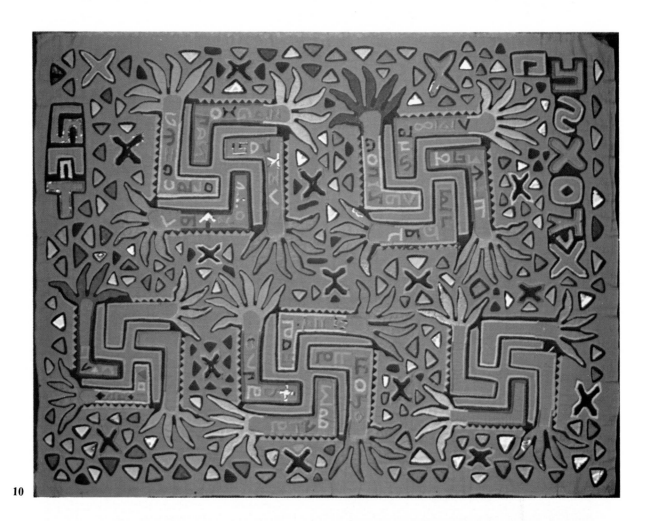

10

11

12

13

14

15

17

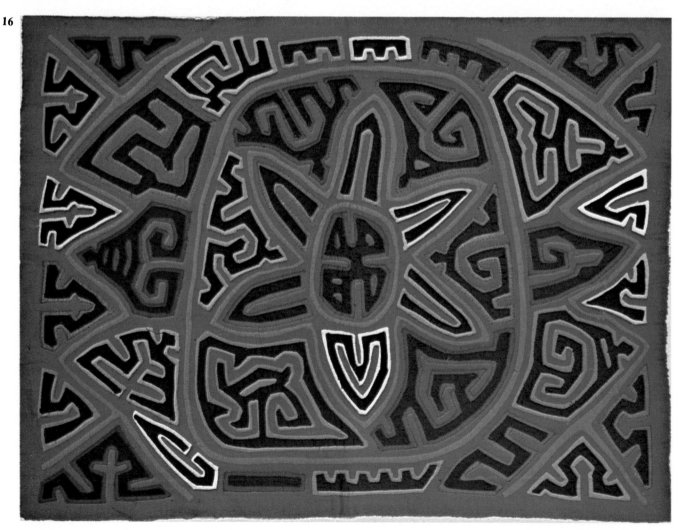

16

18

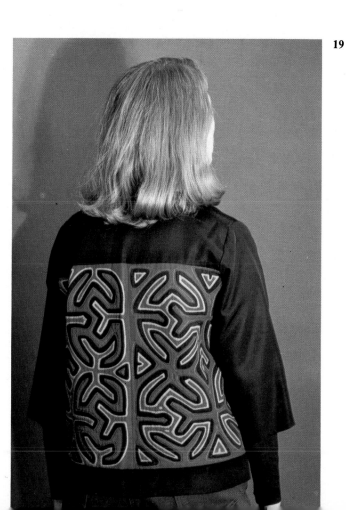
19

20

21

22

23

24

25

Color Plates

Color plate 1. A mola panel with four basic colors, mid-1960s. The multicolor stripe that outlines the shapes reveals that the bottom layer is red, the top one black, and that, sandwiched between them, is a mosaic layer of yellow which underlies the figures, and red, which underlies the surrounding area. Both background and foreground have been filled in largely by means of the slit-and-inlay technique and appliquéd circles on circles. (Courtesy of Bill Dragovan.)

Color plate 2. Another four-color mola panel, early 1970s. The bottom layer is black, the top red. Green underlies the large figures and yellow the background. The green middle layer under two tail feathers has been replaced with yellow or orange. The small central figure and the wings are primarily appliqué. (Courtesy of Wilma Birkeland.)

Color plates 3 and 4. Front and back of the same mola blouse, late 1950s or early 1960s. These are both four-color panels with red bottom layers and black top layers. In color plate 3, boats and fish are underlaid with yellow and the background area with orange. In color plate 4, these colors are reversed because the discarded parts of the central layer in the first mola were used for the second. An unusual amount of running stitch embroidery has been added. Differences between front and back are here largely differences in embroidery. In the first panel, for instance, the fish has not yet been caught, and in the second it has. (Courtesy of the Field Museum of Natural History, Chicago, Illinois.)

Color plate 5. A Cuna woman and her baby, 1960s. All of the woman's clothing, including the hand appliquéd mola panel, is made from machine-manufactured cotton goods imported into San Blas. (Courtesy of Susan B. Black. Photograph by Keith M. Black.)

Color plate 6. Mola blouse, early 1970s. Yoke and sleeves are one cotton print, the binding at the bottom another. (Courtesy of the University of Illinois, School of Human Resources and Family Studies.)

Color plate 7. Mola blouse with velveteen yoke and sleeves, late 1950s or early 1960s. Several appliqué lines are regularly placed immediately above the mola panel. Often they are sawtoothed and sometimes rickrack is substituted. (Courtesy of the Field Museum of Natural History, Chicago, Illinois.)

Color plate 8. Mola panel, early 1920s. Early panels are characterized by wide lines, the frequent use of printed fabric, and much piecing of material. (Courtesy of Martha P. Davenport.)

Color plate 9. Mola panel. There are many versions of this popular design of stylized flowers. (Courtesy of the Field Museum of Natural History, Chicago, Illinois.)

Color plate 10. An unusual and striking mola panel based on Indian symbolism, late 1950s or early 1960s. (Courtesy of the Field Museum of Natural History, Chicago, Illinois.)

Color plate 11. Mola panel, early 1970s. Birds, fish, and animals are favorite subjects for molas. (Courtesy of John Birkeland.)

Color plate 12. Back panel of mola, late 1950s or early 1960s. This is almost an exact duplicate of the panel on the front of the blouse except that, here, the word "Ovaltine" is backwards, so that one has the impression that one is looking through an empty bottle to the printing on the front. The inconsistencies are typical: the "v" that is turned upside down, and the word "botella" which reads forward on both front and back panels. Cuna women frequently copy advertisements, canned goods labels, etc. in their molas. (Courtesy of the Field Museum of Natural History, Chicago, Illinois.)

Color plate 13. Mola panel, late 1950s or early 1960s. In Cuna legend, deer bring babies and deposit them in the mothers' hammocks. However, the Cuna are hardly parochial about this, for there are also molas that show the stork at the same work. In this blouse, the colors in the top layer of the panel on the other side are reversed and the deer are black and the background red. (Courtesy of the Field Museum of Natural History, Chicago, Illinois.)

Color plate 14. Mola panel, early 1970s. Graphic motion is very evident in this panel. The panel used on the other side of the same blouse is shown in black-and-white in the frontispiece. (Courtesy of Wilma Birkeland.)

Color plate 15. Mola panel, late 1950s or early 1960s. Despite the unusual number of colors in the wide line that outlines the main figure, this is only a four-color mola, for the innermost yellow line and the outermost blue line are appliqué laid over the red top layer. Green fabric underlies the figure and orange the background. (Courtesy of the Field Museum of Natural History, Chicago, Illinois.)

Color plate 16. Mola panel, mid-1960s. This unusual and striking panel seems to have only two basic layers. (Courtesy of Mary Piunti.)

Color plate 17. Mola panel, early 1970s, 5 × 8 inches. This panel consists of only two layers, black over yellow. The details are appliqué and embroidery. Slit-and-inlay fills the background. Children are taught mola-making through small projects such as this. (Courtesy of Virginia M. Flanagan.)

Color plate 18. Satin wall bas-relief in reverse appliqué and trapunto, by Joan Michaels-Paque, 5½ feet long × 32 inches high. (Courtesy of the artist. Photograph by Hank Paque.)

Color plate 19. Two molas, seamed together down the back of the garment, have been used. The seam joins two molas with reversed colors. (Courtesy of Lillian Brulc.)

Color plate 20. The mola strips were specially made in Panama for this skirt. The top and stole were designed and sewn by the owner. (Courtesy of Josephine Vargas.)

Color plate 21. *Christmas.*
Color plate 22. *Lent.*
Color plate 23. *Pentecost.*
Three banners by Lillian Brulc which are a direct study of the mola. (Courtesy of the Parish Church of Cristo Redentor, San Miguelito, Panama. Photographs by the Reverend John Enright.)

Color plate 24. Tea cozy, by Vivian Poon, reverse appliqué and embroidery. (Courtesy of the artist.)

Color plate 25. *Kaleidoscope*, by Martha Davenport. In this reverse appliqué, the bottom layer is separated from the others. (Courtesy of the artist.)

MOLAS

What They Are · How to Make Them
Ideas They Suggest for Creative Appliqué

RHODA L. AULD

Photographs by Lawrence Auld

VAN NOSTRAND REINHOLD COMPANY
New York   Cincinnati   Toronto   London   Melbourne

In memory of Marjorie Rhind

Also by the author:
Tatting: The contemporary art of knotting with a shuttle (1974)

Photographs by Lawrence Auld except those from the Organization of American States, The Library of Congress, and museums other than the Field Museum of Natural History.

Drawings of Cuna Indians by Lillian Brulc
All other drawings by Jill Nordfors with the exception of Figures 1-1, 1-2, 3-6, 3-12, 3-14, 3-16—3-21, 6-3, 6-4, and 6-7, which are by Henry Castillo.

Printed in The United States
Designed by Loudan Enterprises

Published in 1977 by Van Nostrand Reinhold Company
A division of Litton Educational Publishing, Inc.
450 West 33rd Street, New York, NY 10001, U.S.A.

Van Nostrand Reinhold Limited
1410 Birchmount Road, Scarborough, Ontario M1P 2E7, Canada

Van Nostrand Reinhold Australia Pty. Limited
17 Queen Street, Mitcham, Victoria 3132, Australia

Van Nostrand Reinhold Company Limited
Molly Millars Lane, Wokingham, Berkshire, England

16 15 14 13 12 11 10 9 8 7 6 5 4 3 2 1

Library of Congress Cataloging in Publication Data

Auld, Rhoda L
  Molas.

  Bibliography: p.
  Includes index.
    1. Appliqué. 2. Molas. 3. Cuna Indians—
Textile industry and fabrics. I. Title.
TT779.A84   746.4   76-17156
ISBN 0-442-20379-9

Guide to Pronunciation

Mola—Moe-lah
Cuna—Coo-nah
San Blas—Sahn Blahs

Drawings of Cuna Indians by Lillian Brulc.

Frontispiece: Mola panel, early 1970s, the mate to the one shown in color in color plate C-14. (Courtesy of Wilma Birkeland)

Contents

Preface

Molas, the colorful appliqué panels created by the Cuna Indians, almost all of whom live in the San Blas Territory of Panama, are unique. Similar needlework is not to be found anywhere else in the world, even among neighboring Indian tribes with related cultures. A good many misconceptions are held about these handmade molas, especially in the United States where much that is incorrect has been written about them in popular literature. It has been said, for instance, that they go back to antiquity. Yet they are a modern invention, never having been made of anything except machine-manufactured cloth secured by the Cuna through trade channels that became well-established only in the mid-1800s. The less complex forms of the art go back not much further than the beginning of this century while the more elaborate kinds date from about the 1940s. The craft represents, in fact, the adaptation to its own needs, by a nonindustrial people, of imported, mass-produced goods.

This book looks at molas, their history, and the Indians who make them primarily from the point of view of the contemporary craftsman, and, although there can be no attempt here to catalog designs, much of the information in the book ought to be of interest to collectors as well. The later chapters describe in detail how to construct the panels, and it will come as a surprise to some, but not to all, that the method shown is quite different from "reverse appliqué," which, for over a decade, has been widely believed to be the mola-making process but which is really a gross oversimplification of what the Cuna women do. The authentic mola technique is almost pure appliqué, although it is true that the Indians begin their work by stacking up several layers of cloth.

Nevertheless, reverse appliqué is not ignored here. Born in an attempt to explain how to make a mola, the concept was a happy accident which resulted in a brand new challenge for craftsmen. Reverse appliqué is described in detail in Chapter 5, as an art related to the authentic mola technique and as an equally fertile source of ideas for modern artists.

My thanks to all those who answered inquiries, volunteered information, translated letters, loaned photographs, or allowed their possessions to be photographed, especially if it consumed their time or involved packing and shipping. Special thanks to former Peace Corps volunteers once stationed in San Blas; to Lillian Brulc; to those connected with the Church of Cristo Redentor, San Miguelito, Panama, who assisted so generously; to Denise Bein for posing for pictures; and to the staff of the Department of Anthropology of the Field Museum of Natural History, Chicago, Illinois, for their extraordinary courtesy.

Photographs by the Reverend John Enright were taken in 1976. The illustrations in Figures 2-6 and 2-7 are reproduced from Lionel Wafer, *A New Voyage and Description of the Isthmus of America* . . . (London: Printed for J. Knapton, 1699). The map in Figure 1-1 is based on one in *Area Handbook for Panama*, DA Pam 550-46, by Thomas E. Weil et al (Washington, D.C.: GPO, 1972). The map in Figure 1-2 is adapted from *Panama: Plano de la Ciudad de Panama y Mapa de Carreteras* (Panama City: Odin Rente un Auto, 1974).

Urbana, Illinois
April, 1976

San Blas woman in gala dress, 1955.

1.

The Land and the People of the Mola

The mola vibrates with color. Its beauty and visual sophistication have enchanted craftsmen, and its technical complexity has baffled them. Yet this distinctive art form is the product of a relatively simple and isolated society. For the mola-makers are the Cuna Indians that live in the remote San Blas Territory of Eastern Panama.

Many people who have seen molas—even some who own them—have vague or inaccurate notions about the Cuna, or no idea at all. We begin, therefore, with a short study of the Indians and their homeland.

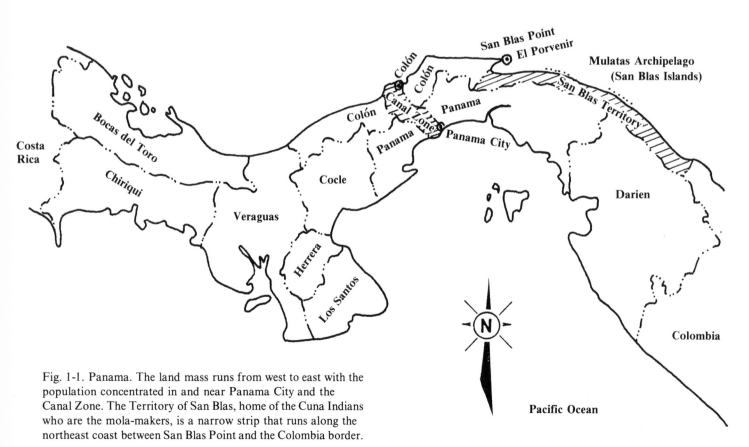

Fig. 1-1. Panama. The land mass runs from west to east with the population concentrated in and near Panama City and the Canal Zone. The Territory of San Blas, home of the Cuna Indians who are the mola-makers, is a narrow strip that runs along the northeast coast between San Blas Point and the Colombia border.

Eastern Panama and San Blas

People generally think of Panama as running from north to south, but a look at the map (fig. 1-1) shows that its length actually lies from west to east. Most of the eastern third, which begins immediately beyond the suburbs of Colón and Panama City, is the region of Darien, and it includes part of Panama Province as well as all of Darien Province. It consists chiefly of thick virgin forest and swamp and is so sparsely populated that it contains less than 2 percent of the country's people. The low mountains that rise above the jungle to form the area's backbone grow higher as you go east until they reach about 6,000 feet near the Colombian border. They slope down to coastal plains on both the Atlantic and Pacific sides.

Innumerable small rivers flow from the mountains to the sea. An average of 130 inches of rain falls annually on the Atlantic side, where the rainy season is nine months long in some places. The steamy tropical climate is more pleasant in the Pacific area, which is somewhat drier. Overland transportation is almost nonexistent here where even the last section of the Pan-American Highway still defies construction. People travel by way of dugout canoe or Indian foot trail.

The San Blas Territory is on the Atlantic side of this wild region. It consists of the long, narrow strip between the Caribbean and the continental divide, and it includes the more than 365 tiny islands of the Mulatas Archipelago that dot the water for 100 miles between San Blas Point, near where the island of El Porvenir is located, and the Colombian border (fig. 1-2). The islands are scattered in a wide band anywhere from 1 to 10 miles from shore. Almost all of them are low-lying coral formations, and they are sheltered from the ocean's turbulence by a long barrier reef.

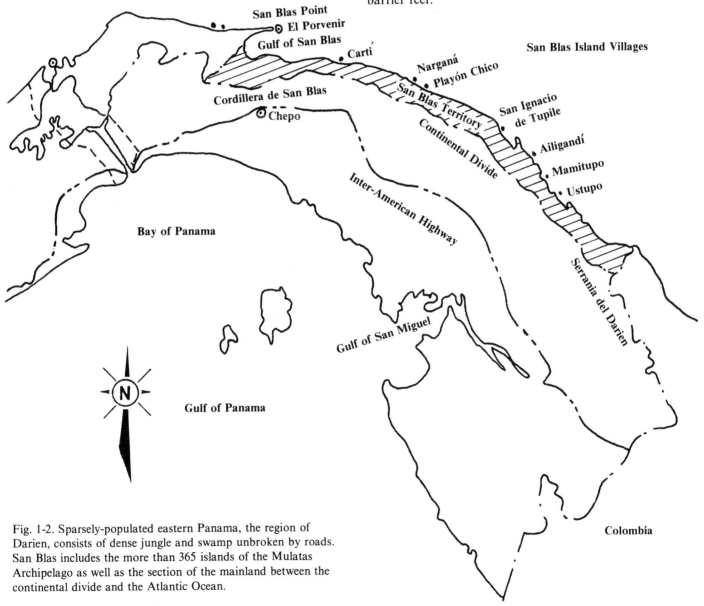

Fig. 1-2. Sparsely-populated eastern Panama, the region of Darien, consists of dense jungle and swamp unbroken by roads. San Blas includes the more than 365 islands of the Mulatas Archipelago as well as the section of the mainland between the continental divide and the Atlantic Ocean.

The thatched houses of the San Blas Cuna Indians stand in crowded communities on about 40 of the islands that are nearest the shore and opposite the mouths of mainland rivers upon which the people depend for fresh water and thoroughfare by dugout canoe to their small mainland farms. The Indians are known to the outside world as Cuna, but strictly speaking, Cuna is the name of their language only and they call themselves *Tule*, which means "men" or "people." In 1970, there were estimated to be almost 25,000 Cuna altogether. There is also an insignificant number of Cuna living elsewhere in Panama and in Colombia. In addition to their own language, Spanish is widespread among them and some speak English.

San Blas is nominally under the jurisdiction of the republic of Panama, but the Indians have almost complete autonomy and make and enforce their own laws through their tribal chiefs and town councils in which every adult male is represented. The Territory is essentially a reservation in the sense that it is set aside for exclusive use by the Cuna. Sale of land is forbidden to outsiders and settlement there or leasehold for commercial purposes is permitted only with the Indians' consent. The inhabitants are not restricted to this area, though most choose to remain in order to preserve their tribal ways.

The region is less than a hundred miles from Panama's urban centers of Colón and Panama City. Outsiders reach it primarily by small plane, and there are regular flights which take less than thirty minutes, but, in general, only those who make a special effort to get there visit this out-of-the-way place. They are chiefly the dwindling number of traders who call periodically in their small boats, but who meet more and more competition from Indian enterprise, and an increasing number of tourists who are now encouraged by a growing portion of the community.

Cuna History

Traditionally, as a direct result of their contacts with the conquistadors in the sixteenth century, the Cuna have guarded their tribal ways against the encroachments of modern civilization by means of a fierce exclusiveness, and it should be noted that a portion of the population still supports this concept. Until relatively recently, most visitors other than the traders were not entirely welcome, almost nobody was allowed to stay overnight in the Territory, and native women were forbidden to set foot outside it under pain of death. But this should not lead one to believe that the Indians have lived in isolation. For nearly five centuries, they have been in constant contact

Fig. 1-3. Cuna Indian family, 1975. The boy wears a fertility necklace of animal teeth. (Courtesy of the Organization of American States.)

12

with people of European and African origin who have moved in around their homeland. The Cuna have been suspicious of these strangers and, in contrast with most other Panamanians who are of mixed white, Negro, and Indian ancestry, have virtually never intermarried with them. On the other hand, they have made and are still making changes in their own culture as a result of their encounters with these other groups, and they have always been most interested in trading with them. Moreover, Cuna men have worked on foreign ships since the seventeenth or eighteenth centuries, going all round the world, and large numbers of them, especially the young, leave their homes and families for prolonged periods to work or go to school in Panama's cities or the Canal Zone.

Until about the middle of the nineteenth century, the Cuna lived not on the islands but on the mainland. Their houses stood along the rivers where the best farmlands are found. They raised just enough food for their needs and rounded out their diet with game. But small foreign boats had begun to frequent San Blas. They traded with the inhabitants on a regular basis for their coconuts, which grew wild along the shore and on the archipelago, and for tortoise shell which, for many years, and especially in the 1920s, was almost as important an item of exchange as the coconut. The removal to the coast was primarily in response to this growing commerce, which eventually made coconuts virtually identical with money in San Blas, especially after 1870 when some groups began to plant and cultivate more groves. A tidal wave which wiped out many of the mainland homes at the edges of the rivers caused more people to relocate and all but a very small number of the Indians settled on the islands. From their new place of residence, the Indians could make daily trips to the mainland in dugout canoes to cultivate their crops with primitive instruments, wash themselves and their clothes, and obtain the necessary supplies of fresh water and firewood, which are not available on the islands. Their new location also made it easier for them to oversee their coconut groves and to catch turtles on the uninhabited outer islands.

Earlier, such a move would not have been possible, for, almost from the day that Columbus explored and named San Blas in 1502, Darien became the scene of a 300-year struggle between the Indians and Spanish colonists. Attracted by the gold in its numerous small mines, the conquistadors built their first settlement there in 1510. At that time, the direct ancestors of today's Cuna probably lived close to what is now the Colombian border on the north side of the Isthmus. They were part of a larger group, the Caribe-Cuna, that numbered over 700,000 and whose territory was all of eastern Panama. Here, as elsewhere in the New World, the Spaniards, despite the remonstrances of King and Church, displayed their total disregard for the humanity and civilization of the friendly Indians, who had a complex social organization far more elaborate than that of today's Cuna. Their numbers cut down to only about 10,000 by the diseases of the Europeans as well as by slaughter and the rigors of slavery in the gold mines, the surviving Indians disappeared into inaccessible mountain regions from where they could wage war against the intruders. To this day, stories of the atrocities of the Spaniards and their bloody missionary zeal are carried down in the Cuna's chants and legends and color their attitude toward Spanish Panama.

The towns that the Spanish colonists built in Panama formed the western end of the Spanish Main. Corsairs and buccaneers, beginning with Britain's Sir Francis Drake, quickly moved in to attack these settlements and their shipping in the undeclared war between England and its European allies against Spain for the domination of the New World. The San Blas Islands were a favorite hideout for the pirate ships. The Cuna, though wary of all Europeans after their experiences with the Spanish, joined with the raiders against the common enemy, acting as guides across the Isthmus and providing food for the sailors. One result of this coalition was to lessen the intense antagonism on the part of the Indians toward nonSpanish-speaking Europeans, especially the English, an attitude which persisted for centuries.

Shifting European relationships caused the abrupt decline of piracy shortly before 1700, but warfare between the natives and the Spanish colonists, continually aggravated by encouragement of the Indians' hostility by such interested parties as the governments of nearby British colonies, endured until the beginning of the nineteenth century when economic and other changes lessened outside interest in Darien, and the colonial government recognized the Cuna's independence. Though they came out of the centuries of strife many fewer in number and vastly changed in social organization, and with more changes still to come with their new life in the islands, these people were one of the very few native groups that emerged from the period of Spanish dominance essentially unconquered.

The Indians and the Islands

The Cuna are remarkable for their short stature. Normally brown-skinned, they have the world's highest rate of albinism. The men wear modern dress, some of it home-made. Most of the women wear nose rings. Their distinctive costume, of which the mola forms a part, will be described in the next chapter. Both men and women usually go barefoot in their homeland, but sandals of various sorts are now worn by some. Most girls dress like replicas of their mothers, but the very tiny ones may be clothed in anything from purchased clothing to only jewelry. All boys used to wear nothing except virility necklaces of animal teeth, but shirts and shorts are now quite common, especially among school children. Birds and monkeys are kept as pets, as well as cats and dogs.

The islands on which the Indians live vary in size. A few are so small they have room for only a few houses. The villages are laid out along broad, unpaved streets. Most dwellings are rectangular structures with thatched roofs, and can be as large as 50 feet in length. Their windowless walls are made of stakes, usually cane, set close to each other. There are no interior partitions although there may be a loft at one end. All construction is fastened together entirely with split vines. The floors are usually packed sand, although concrete is becoming popular. Most households have two buildings; one for sleeping and a smaller cookhouse where food is prepared over a chimneyless log fire. Very large families may also have more than one sleeping house. Outhouses are built over the water and are often shared by more than one family. The interiors of the homes are neatly kept, and the sparse furniture, some of it merely packing boxes, consists of tables, a few hand-made stools and benches, storage chests and shelves. Hammocks are used for sleeping though there is an occasional bed. Lighting is by kerosene lamp. But, as anyone who has lived in the tropics or sub-tropics knows, houses of thatch and cane must be renewed constantly and they attract vermin. In the last decade, therefore, structures of reinforced concrete with galvanized iron roofs have been introduced, and most of the islands now have one or more, some of which are private residences.

Almost every village has its general store that is run by

Fig. 1-4. Cuna women and children in a San Blas village. The light-skinned girl in the center is an albino. (Courtesy of the Organization of American States.)

an individual Cuna or by a group of them. Once these outlets got most of their stock from the trading boats, but, more and more, they are supplied by local enterprise directly from Colón. There are schools on more than half of the islands and a very few Christian churches. One church complex includes a hospital, and a few government clinics are located elsewhere. With the new interest in tourism, a few tourist accommodations have appeared, and they are run by the Indians themselves or by outsiders with Cuna consent, but there is strong objection to the nonIndian facilities on the part of the more conservative section of the population.

The Cuna learn to swim as soon as they can walk, and *cayucos* or dugout canoes are their means of transportation not only for the daily trips to the mainland but to Colón as well. The boats vary in size from those that fathers make for their small children to the large seagoing sailing canoes that are taken as much as 75 miles out to sea. The large native mahogany trees from which these dugouts once were made are now scarce, and the Indians buy unfinished canoes from Colombia. Another innovation in the last decade is the use of cooperatively-bought and -operated motor boats which carry passengers and freight between San Blas and the cities.

Fig. 1-5. Cuna mothers and children, 1960. (Courtesy of Braniff Airways.)

Fig. 1-6. The Cuna houses and the coconut groves seem to overburden the small, low-lying islands on which they stand. The Indians depend on dugout canoes for transportation. (Courtesy of the photographer, the Reverend John Enright.)

Agriculture, Food and Daily Life

Land in San Blas is poor except near the rivers, where most cultivation takes place. Two crops are often gathered in a year. The Indians' method of tillage is a slash-and-burn technique that goes back before Columbus. Although farms are owned by individuals, this kind of agriculture requires help, especially when clearing or harvesting, and the men cooperate with each other. One person's farmlands, by the way, may be widely scattered, and there are plots that are distant enough from the islands to require an overnight stay. The general lack of transportation in all of Panama creates a situation in which the cities can import foreign produce more cheaply than that which is raised in their own country. As a result, there are few large-scale agricultural operations and farmers largely grow food for their own use.

The reader should keep in mind that the Cuna Indians' standard of living compares very favorably with that of the rest of rural Panama, which comprises 50 percent of that country's population. Few of these farmers are needy, but most live in thatched houses with dirt floors and no plumbing or electricity. Their sparse furniture is augmented with packing boxes, and they cook in separate buildings over open fires. Unlike the Cuna, most rent

their land or are squatters, but they, too, travel Panama's rivers by dugout canoe, live on what they raise with primitive tools on their couple of acres, buy few manufactured goods, often resist modern medical care even though it is available, and have had limited educational opportunities. Cuna life is hardly unique in these respects. However, many aspects of it are distinctive, such as the women's costume and the group's trading and seafaring skills, and not found even among the country's two other major Indian groups, the closely-related Chocó who live elsewhere in Darien (and also in Colombia), and the Guaymi of western Panama.

As in most agricultural communities, the Indians' day begins very early. The men farm, fish, build and repair houses, boats, and paths, and fill in the edges of the islands with landfill from the mainland. A few work for other farmers for pay or have civil service or other non-agricultural jobs. The women wash clothes, fetch water, and prepare the food. Mola-making is a spare time activity and many Cuna women devote all of their leisure hours to it. Traditionally, men sew their clothing and that of their sons, and the women their own, but this is not a hard and fast rule. Hand-operated sewing machines are used by men and women alike to make men's pants and shirts and sometimes to put together the women's blouses

Fig. 1-7. A view of an Indian village. The houses are laid out along unpaved streets. (Courtesy of Wilma Birkeland. Reproduced from a color slide taken by C. J. Birkeland.)

after the panels are completed by hand. Most of the men's crafts, basketry, for example, are leisure time activities since the men are away from home working during a good part of the day.

Work is over by midday when the big meal is served. The men eat first. The Cuna's primary staple is the plantain, or cooking banana. Rice, the chief food of Panama, is also an important part of their diet, and they hull it in enormous wooden mortars that rest on the ground. Two women alternate strokes with huge pestles, also of wood. Other starchy foods are corn, manioc, yams, and increasingly, wheat bread, which involves purchase. Since moving to the islands, fish has been eaten rather than the small game the men used to shoot. To replace the meat in their diets, more and more people are keeping pigs and chickens, although they were once raised only for trade or ceremonial use. Fruits cultivated and eaten include pineapples, citrus fruits, mangoes, papayas, guavas, and avocados. Food is boiled, baked, and sometimes smoked. Increasingly, canned fish, rice, sugar, soft drinks, and even extra bananas are bought from the island stores. Coconuts are little used for food, perhaps because of their important role in the economy. Water is seldom drunk. Instead, thick, hot drinks made of mixtures of sugar cane, cacao, and grain or mashed plantains are kept bubbling in kettles.

Fig. 1-9. Cuna house. The walls are stakes, usually of cane, set close to each other. All construction is fastened together with split vines. (Courtesy of the photographer, the Reverend John Enright.)

Fig. 1-8. A house under construction. (Courtesy of the photographer, the Reverend John Enright.)

Native Crafts vs. Trade Goods

Before the Spaniards came, the Cuna had stone implements, and the use of metal did not become widespread among them until the beginning of the eighteenth century. Today, they tend to prefer trade goods such as commercial fishhooks, machetes, buckets, string and rope, combs, and so forth, to their own handicrafts which are rapidly diminishing. Calabashes with single small holes at the top are still depended upon to carry water, along with more modern devices, and these gourds have other uses as well. Wood-carving continues to be practiced by the men, who produce wooden medicine dolls or images of various sizes, the smallest of which are amulets worn round childrens' necks, reed flutes, staffs of office for the chief men, one-piece stools, bowls, and plates. Basketry is on the decline, though fire fans continue to be braided. The potter's art virtually died out with the advent of the traders in the middle of the nineteenth century. Growing, spinning, and dyeing cotton are lost skills, and weaving survives only in the making of ceremonial hammocks. This craft too is at an end, and almost all hammocks are now purchased from Colombia. Another handicraft that has virtually expired is the creation of feather cloth which was much like that made by the Hawaiians. Besides hand-operated sewing machines, many people own and use battery-operated radios, etc.

Fig. 1-10. Two Indian women paddle a *cayuco* or dugout canoe. Notice the turtle's head carving on the prow. (Courtesy of the photographer, the Reverend John Enright.)

Fig. 1-11. Hulling rice. This is the traditional method, but, increasingly, rice is bought in the stores. Notice the unfinished mola in the woman's left hand. These women are undoubtedly performing for tourists. (Courtesy of the photographer, the Reverend John Enright.)

18

The Family

Cuna marriages are arranged by the fathers of the young couple, usually when the boy is about nineteen years old and the girl about sixteen or seventeen. Generally, it is the bride's parent who makes the initial advance. The boy is not often consulted, and the marriage ceremony consists of kidnapping him and throwing him into the girl's hammock three nights in a row. Few young men who are thus chosen are allowed to escape.

For the bridegroom, the price of marriage is agricultural service to his wife's family. The young man goes to live with them in a household that may number considerably more than ten people. The extended family, or clan, is ruled over by the oldest couple and consists of all their joint progeny except for married men who have gone to live elsewhere. The family may also include younger sisters of the oldest woman and their spouses and offspring. A divorce, and they are common, or the death of a wife, releases the husband from his wife's household, but his children remain there. Remarriages are arranged by the two people involved with the consent of the community. Nowadays, although extended families are still the rule, they tend to be smaller than formerly and, increasingly, money is substituted for service to the father-in-law, who himself often encourages his daughters' husbands to take jobs for pay.

In spite of this matrilocal setup, it is the men who rule Cuna life. Women are considered to be not quite as intelligent though they are allowed to own and inherit property, which their men cultivate for them. The male head of the clan is absolute ruler over the members of his household. His sons-in-law work for him until he dies, when they may elect to leave and set up their own homes or to stay together, in which case the oldest surviving male takes over.

The agricultural work is assigned daily by the head man. His permission is required before his younger subordinates can go to take care of their own property (every child is given at least some coconut trees at birth) or to aid their own relatives with whom they maintain reciprocal ties, since property is inherited from generation to generation or by siblings and is never left to a spouse. The women's daily duties are assigned and overseen by the head woman.

Fig. 1-12. Women dancing, an important part of the girl's puberty ceremony. The "rehearsal" here is probably for the benefit of tourists. Reed Pan's pipes and gourd rattles are about all that survive of traditional musical instruments. The women have removed their headscarves to reveal their closely cropped hair. The Cuna men and children wear store-bought clothes. (Courtesy of the photographer, the Reverend John Enright.)

Government

Government is mainly local and centered in the town council. Each community has its council house, usually a separate building, where the men meet almost daily under the leadership of their chief to discuss business. Traditionally, this included religious concerns as well as assignment to the various households of the work shared by the entire male populace, the administration of justice, and relationships with other villages and the world at large. Today, two chiefs may be chosen. One is the traditional "singing" chief whose sphere is the religion, morals, and cultural heritage of his people. The other presides over purely secular business meetings, the interests of which have been expanded to include mail, rural electrification, and the building of airports. Standing committees handle much of the work in this new type of meeting and, in a few places, the women participate and vote along with the men.

The household heads are expected to keep the members of their clan in line, but if they cannot, or in a quarrel between two families, disputes are settled and punishment meted out by popular vote of the entire community. Traditionally, even capital crimes, including those against the tribe like bearing children of mixed blood, were handled by the Indians themselves, but today, the Panama government is called in when murder, arson, or grand theft are committed. Village policemen keep order, summon people to meetings, greet and cater to visitors, and collect food for feasts.

Government above the local level is weakened by factions, but general congresses to which the various local meetings send representatives are held several times a year. The high chiefs who preside are merely village chiefs who wield a little more influence than the others. They also head the delegations of Indians that negotiate treaties with the government of Panama. The Territory falls under the jurisdiction of the Indian Affairs Department of the federal Ministry of Government and Justice, which is also responsible for similar, though smaller, Indian territories in western Panama. The San Blas Territory is considered part of Colón Province. The local arm of the government is the *Intendencia*, or provincial governor's office, located on El Porvenir.

Religion and Medicine

Although Panama is now committed to a policy of religious freedom, it made determined efforts in the early days of the Republic to convert the Cuna to Roman Catholicism, the state religion until 1923. Considerable inroads were made around Narganá where, in the first quarter of this century, many of the people were won not only to the new belief but to modern dress as well. Protestants have also made some gains, and their headquarters are at Ailigandí.

Most of the Cuna, however, continue to follow their ancestral faith though they have modified it extensively. They believe in a remote Creator to whom one does not pray or sacrifice but who made the world and everything in it including the sixteen levels of the Underworld and the Heaven above, hosts of minor spirits and demons, who must be dealt with through chants and magic. The Creator made his own wife, too, who gave birth to man and several animals and plants as well. He also sent heroes to earth whose task it was to teach man morals and culture. The most important of these showed him how to build their houses and to spin, weave, and dye. He indicated which work should be done by men and which by women, and he made the first nose rings, which were originally worn by both men and women.

Since the Indians believe that non-living things and the forces of nature possess spirits or souls, many of which are evil, much of the religious business of the community has to do with appeasing or outwitting these forces. In addition, good spirits can be trapped in wooden images. These *uchus* are figurines in the shape of men, women, or animals. They often show borrowings from other cultures, such as the top hat.

Fig. 1-13. *Uchu.* (Courtesy of Lillian Brulc.)

The chief and the medicine man are the most important religious figures. Both undergo long years of apprenticeship to a series of older practitioners. The chief, having learned his trade, which includes at least a little knowledge of the lore of the medicine man and the other religious leaders, is chosen by popular male vote. Generally he serves for life though he may step down because of old age or other cause. He calls the people to the council house almost every night ahd chants, often in a language that must be translated by his assistants. His knowledge today is by no means as extensive as was that of his predecessors and much of the tribe's oral tradition is being lost, though a few incantations have been written down in picture writing. The chief keeps the people conversant with their religious heritage and their past and gives them moral guidance according to their traditions. He tries to stop trouble before it starts, especially where women and children are concerned, by lecturing them, in special sessions, on how to behave. In the case of the children, punishment is also meted out weekly.

There are a variety of medicine men, some of whom specialize in epidemics, but the most numerous are the *inatuledis* who doctor the individuals of the community. Their stock-in-trade includes chants, *uchus*, special staffs, herbs and other primitive medicines such as powdered charcoal believed to prevent the birth of albinos, and ground animal pelvic bones believed to insure easy childbirth.

Fig. 1-15. Cuna staff. Hand-carved wooden staffs serve as badges of office for Cuna officials. (Courtesy of Lillian Brulc.)

Fig. 1-14. Cuna pictograph: "Funeral Ceremony and Journey of the Soul." (Courtesy of the Smithsonian Institution, National Anthropological Archives.)

Making modern medical care available to rural areas in a country hampered by lack of transportation is a major concern of the Panamanian government and much progress has been made in the first half of the seventies. The Cuna cooperated with them in the decade between 1955 and 1965 to effect a huge drop in deaths from tuberculosis in San Blas. Most of the Indians believe illness to have supernatural as well as natural causes and they tend to patronize both tribal doctors and modern physicians. There is also a portion of the population that resorts to patent medicines which are cheaper than either doctors or *inatuledis*, both of whom demand payment in cash and will not accept coconuts in return for most of their ministrations. Infant death is high among the Cuna and, in the late 1960s, the mortality rates in childbirth were about one-third of the total birth rate.

Indian burial follows a full day and a night of mourning. The corpse, dressed in its best clothes and tied in a hammock, is rowed to the mainland where it is interred with gravegoods believed to be needed in the afterlife. Nowadays, not as many possessions are left with the body as formerly. Valuables are removed and many objects are broken to prevent theft. Specially-prepared strings, (probably some kind of looping, since they unravel when pulled) are provided to help the spirit of the deceased find its way. They are now made of commercial string. Souls deserving punishment must proceed through part of the Underworld, but the others go straight to Heaven where they live much as before though in more comfort.

Once, puberty ceremonies for both boys and girls were common. The boy's initiation rite, during the course of which he received his first penis shield, waned in the middle of the nineteenth century, concurrently with a change of male dress as trousers became popular. The girl's ceremony is still widely observed and is a very important village event even though it is becoming more abbreviated. Traditionally the young girl underwent two ceremonies, a simple one at puberty and another, 1 to 5 years later, that lasted 4 days and prepared her for marriage. Now frequently only the 4-day ceremony is observed, during which the young lady is secluded and bathed almost constantly for a period of days. She is daubed all over with a berry juice that turns her an uneven black. The dye, which takes a long time to wear off, is thought to make her un-attractive to evil spirits, to which she is considered particularly vulnerable at this time of her life. Her hair is cut to the short adult length, her fortune is told, and she is given a name. Afterward there is a community feast, including food and drink. Purchased rum has largely replaced the native brew that was carefully fermented from sugar cane and corn or plantains for each ceremony not too long ago.

Preserving Tribal Ways

Relative isolation combined with a workable economic foundation have so far enabled the Cuna to retain their separate identity to the present day. Most want to maintain their tribal way of life, but economic changes make it difficult. Previously, the Cuna could be considered almost wealthy compared to many other Indian groups or groups of farmers in Panama; today there is more and more need for cash, and the younger men prefer to seek it instead of farming or fishing. New sources of income must be found if the Cuna are to continue their political and economic independence, while maintaining and even improving their standard of living. Many of the people of San Blas are looking to increased tourism as the most likely source of new revenue, but public and private business ventures, usually organized as cooperatives, are also multiplying. Airports, stores, trading boats, and commercial agriculture or fishing are some of the undertakings the Indians have embarked upon.

Many young leaders who want to keep their native society intact are devoting themselves to increasing the educational opportunities within San Blas. Though about half the Cuna were literate in Spanish by the late 1960s, and over half the islands had elementary schools, most of them public, there was only one junior high and many children went to Panama City to study. Usually, they expected to remain and work there, and if they returned home, had difficulty in fitting themselves back into the native culture. The young people who want to correct this situation study abroad themselves and return to help establish schools. By 1971, there were several primary and secondary schools on the larger islands that were run by these new teachers.

This, then, is the society that produced the mola.

2.

The Mola and How It Grew

Today, the Cuna man commonly wears an undecorated shirt and trousers, but the woman wears a distinctive and striking costume characterized by an assemblage of patterns and colors. All of the fabric that goes into it, including the mola fabric, is machine-manufactured and obtained by the Indians through trade.

The Cuna Woman's Costume

Four different trade-good cotton prints, two mola panels, and a collection of jewelry combine to make the Cuna woman's outer dress, an example of which is shown in color plate C-5. One print, the headdress, consists of two identical square scarfs which have not been cut apart. It is usually bright red and yellow although the particulars of the design vary. The scarves are ordinary machine yardage with printed designs. Usually there are charming details such as a hen and chicks or a small cart. Adult women wear their hair closely bobbed in back and with straight bangs in front.

The second piece of printed cloth is wrapped around the waist with the end tucked in for a skirt. Once this was always predominantly blue, and that still tends to be the case although other colors are also seen nowadays. The garment reaches to just below the knees and is sometimes longer. It is worn over a short, solid-colored underskirt.

The upper garment is shown by itself in color plates C-6 and C-7. Two mola panels form the lower front and back of this blouse. The term *mola* originally meant *cloth*, although it is now applied to both the blouse and the individual panels. The hand-sewn mola rectangles, made by the women themselves, are almost always fashioned from vivid, solid-colored cottons. They range from simple,

two-color appliqué of a special sort to a very intricate kind that superimposes one fabric upon another in accordance with the rigid scheme described in detail in Chapter 4. Whenever three or more colors are used, the larger scraps left from one panel can be incorporated into a second which is identical with it except that some of the colors will be reversed (see Chapter 4) and the two panels are usually sewn into the same blouse. But even when the technique does not dictate these differences, the front and back designs of a blouse are still never exactly the same. The variation may be very slight, but it is always there. Both design and workmanship in the panels runs the gamut from excellent to very poor. In spite of the care lavished on the appliqué, mola blouses are crudely put together, often with large basting stitches. The panels are seamed to the other pieces of the blouse in the simplest way possible, and the blouse is bound at the bottom.

The often crudely-fashioned yoke to which the mola panels are attached and the short, slightly-puffed sleeves usually account for the third print in the outfit, although they are sometimes made of velveteen which sets off the richness of the needlework beautifully and is more to our taste. The back of the yoke is generally narrowed at the top by means of a large tuck. The front is slit. A drawstring is ordinarily pulled through the narrow neckline binding. The loosely-gathered sleeves are also finished with a narrow binding that seldom matches the one at the neck. The fourth print is used for a border about 1½ inches wide at the bottom of the blouse, but that is generally tucked into the skirt and hidden when the garment is worn. Several horizontal appliqué stripes, one or more with sawtooth edges, almost always appear just above each mola rectangle. Sometimes rickrack is used. Such stripes may also be placed along the shoulders and on the sleeves.

The long strings of small glass trade beads that are wound very tightly around arms and legs add more color to the many-hued array. Figure 2-1 shows how these wide constricting bracelets are pre-assembled on cores made of wood and cloth or rolled-up newspaper so that the geometric patterns which they carry may be worked out before the ornaments are placed on the wearer's limbs. The bracelets are worn permanently and sometimes become quite tight as the wearer grows. Other strands of beads may be hung around the neck in heavy ropes, or there may be, instead, enormous gold-plated pendants, collections of gold coins, or, less often today, strings of natural materials like shells and seeds. In any case, a necklace or collection of necklaces is an integral part of the costume and often they obscure the mola design on the front of the blouse.

Many rings are worn, sometimes more than one to a finger. Earrings are usually gold-plated disks with small pendants attached, the largest the family can afford, and sometimes they are four or five inches in diameter. But the essential piece of jewelry for most Cuna women is a heavy, gold-plated nose ring. Today, however, the custom is beginning to die out and the ornament is seen less and less on the very young. Noses and ears, by the way, are pierced when the baby is only a few days old, and a year-old baby girl with only nose ring and earrings was not an uncommon sight a short time ago. Babies may be painted black like the girl at puberty to ward off evil disease spirits. The Cuna themselves worked gold before the Spanish conquest, but, after their terrible experiences at the hands of the conquistadors, this was outlawed, apparently by the tribe, and today they buy their jewelry.

Fig. 2-1. Cotton prints and beads from the Cuna woman's costume. At the left is the headscarf, two red and yellow squares that have not been cut apart. The skirt, a rectangle that is wrapped around the waist, is at the right. The design in the constricting leg and arm bracelets is worked out first on the wood and cloth cores shown in the center or on rolled up newspapers. (Courtesy of Lillian Brulc.)

24

The Indian woman may paint a narrow straight black line down her nose from just above the bridge to the tip, which seems to be a survival of an earlier custom of painting animal figures head downwards on the nose, and she may redden her cheeks. Commercial cosmetics are now often substituted for the native fruit juices once used exclusively for this decoration, if the marks are made at all.

Fig. 2-2. A pair of Cuna earrings. These are only 1½-inch in diameter, but many are 4 or 5 inches across. The design appears to be lightly stamped into the thin metal. (Courtesy of Wilma Birkeland.)

Fig. 2-3. Half of another red and yellow headscarf. (Courtesy of Wilma Birkeland.)

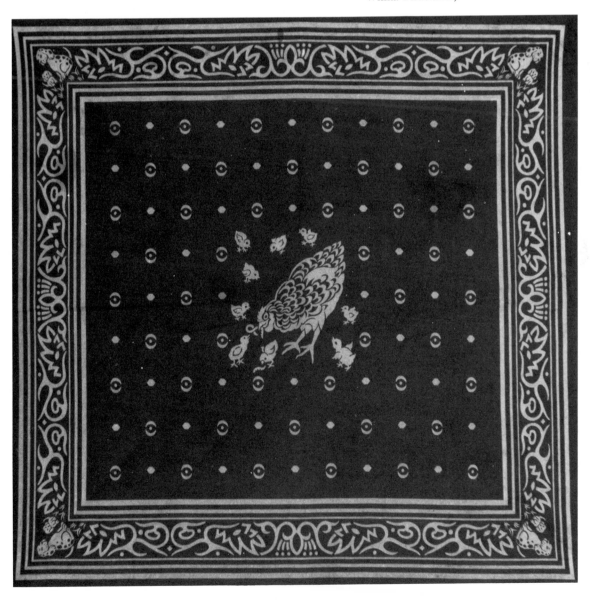

Cuna Dress from the Sixteenth Century to Modern Times

This elaborate costume, depending entirely as it does on the wearer's access to trade goods, did not begin to evolve until the Cuna had moved to the islands in the middle of the nineteenth century. When the Spaniards arrived in the early 1500s, the Darien Indians had a complex social system and the amount of jewelry and cloth that was worn indicated status. At that time the natives raised, spun, and wove a limited supply of cotton fabric, and natural dyes were used to color it. Women, naked above the waist, were clothed in wrap-around skirts that reached to the knees or, for those of highest rank, to the ankles. Men's attire was limited to penis coverings of hard substances such as shell or gold. Both sexes wore ear and nose ornaments, necklaces, and many other kinds of gold jewelry. Body painting and tattooing were both practiced.

Fig. 2-5. San Blas Indian girls, 1931. The reddened cheeks of the girl on the right is another practice that is on its way out. (Courtesy of the Organization of American States.)

Fig. 2-4. San Blas woman in gala dress, 1955. The custom of painting a black line down the nose is beginning to die out. (Courtesy of the Organization of American States.)

26

A century later, the Indians wore simpler jewelry and less of it. Figures 2-6 and 2-7 are illustrations from a seventeenth-century source that shows the nose ornaments, which had apparently become standardized, the women's being large rings that reached their chins, the men's plates that covered the upper lip. Both sexes were adorned with multiple necklaces of shell and glass trade beads. Some women were said to have been bedecked with thirty or more at a time, and the men sported twice that number and added other necklaces of teeth. The women wore bracelets and the chief men earrings and feather headdresses.

The same document, an account by one of the British pirates, a man who was held hostage by the Indians for two years, describes the bright-colored body painting of the era. Red, yellow, and blue were the favorite pigments. They were mixed in an oil base, kept in calabashes, and applied with a stick chewed at one end into a brush. They were fairly permanent and had to wear off. While every part of the body might receive attention, the face especially was decorated with stylized birds, animals, men, trees, and so forth. The figures were of various sizes not necessarily consistent with each other. Tattooing was, by this time, very much on the decline.

Fig. 2-6. A drawing of the Darien Indians from a book published in the seventeenth century. The men's noseplate is shown in the left foreground, the women's nose ring at the right. (Reproduced from the collection of the Library of Congress.)

Figure 2-7, again from the same source, shows the robes sometimes worn by the men. These must have required sewing and, while the skill may have been known before the conquest, the Spaniards are said to have supplied needles to the Indians who learned to do embroidery, an art thought to have died out among them after the flight to the mountains when little clothing was worn.

By the early eighteenth century, some of the Indian women were using trade cloth for their skirts and many of the men who lived near the coast were beginning to dress themselves in shirts and trousers. By the end of the 1860s, all the adult men were clothed in knee-breeches. Shirts were not as universally worn and were made by the Indians themselves. The style preferred then persisted into this century although the other male garments kept pace with changing times. Fedoras also became an integral part of the masculine costume during this period and they were obligatory at all gala events, including social visits. The men's nose rings had by then been discarded although earrings continued to be worn until the early 1920s, and, in a few cases, even later.

The Indians in their Robes in Councel, and Smoaking tobacco after their way.   Place this P. 102.

Fig. 2-7. Another drawing from the same book. (Reproduced from the collection of the Library of Congress.)

Fig. 2-8. Cuna woman and child, 1931. The girl wears the older form of the mola in which the appliqué panel is longer than at present and forms a skirt which begins just below the armpits. (Courtesy of the Organization of American States.)

Fig. 2-9. Mola skirt, early 1920s, 27 inches long. (Photograph courtesy of Museum of the American Indian, Heye Foundation.)

Development of the Mola Blouse

Again by the end of the 1860s, the women were wearing knee-length shifts, probably white, with short sleeves. This was the beginning of the mola. Twenty years later, these garments were reported to be dark blue with a red band at the bottom. Each hid a hand-painted loincloth or underskirt called a *picha makkalet* whose freehand ornamentation was originally made with a black native dye. This was replaced with indigo brought by the traders, and both types of coloring matter were applied with the gnawed stick described above. Gradually the practice of painting the underskirt died out, presumably because indigo became harder and harder to get, and the custom was almost obsolete by the middle of the twentieth century. Some people attach great significance to this design-covered undercloth, considering it to be an intermediate step between body painting and the mola. Of the mola designs, by the way, all native spokesmen have said that they represent nothing more than decoration.

By 1890 or 1900, the cloth traders were offering the Indians a more extensive choice of colors, and the dresses became brighter. The band at the bottom was elaborated into simple appliqué which quickly widened until it reached from just below the armpits to the hem. Though this form persisted in a few places, by 1900 most of the women began wearing the wrap-around skirts of blue printed cotton. The appliquéd chemise was shortened into a blouse, presumably so that the skirt could be displayed. Molas of this period were decorated with beads, shells, and fragments of broken mirror.

Fig. 2-10. Mola skirt, early 1920s, 28¼-inches long. (Photograph courtesy of Museum of the American Indian, Heye Foundation.)

Fig. 2-11. Mola dress for a large woman, early 1920s, 27 inches long. Here again, the mola forms a skirt. (Photograph courtesy of Museum of the American Indian, Heye Foundation.)

Development of the Mola Design

The very first mola panels were of two colors, one of which formed the background for an elaborate line design cut from the other. Once the idea of adding a third color was conceived of, it took no great ingenuity to add more (see Chapter 4), and the mola in Figure 2-12, known to have been made before 1919, has six. The lines in the early molas were often broad and, even in the same piece, the widths of these varied greatly as though there was a groping for form. Today, if a Cuna woman makes a panel with wide lines, the others ridicule her and call it a "grandmother mola," the implication being that the maker's eyesight must be bad. Another characteristic of the early work is a greater use of patterned rather than plain cloth, especially in the bottom layer. The earliest molas did not depict objects.

The mola in color plate C-8 was brought back from Panama in the first half of the 1920s. It consists basically of four colors. Birds are the subject, and the slit-and-inlay technique (see Chapter 4) has been used. The lines are wide. The colors are relatively dull, although that could be the result of fading. Some of the fabric appears to be coarse silk or an early form of rayon. A great deal of printed cloth has been used which tends to detract from the total effect, and it might have been better had it been limited to the bottom layer. As in many early molas, there is much piecing and one gets the impression that the Indian women at that time used whatever goods they could come by. Figure 2-13, for instance, shows the front of a baby's blouse which was made no later than 1919. The yellow background seems to have been not quite enough for two rectangles, however, and, though not visible in the photograph, a wide vertical stripe of white was substituted for it at the left edge of the panel that forms the back.

Fig. 2-12. A six-color mola made before 1919. (Courtesy of the Field Museum of Natural History, Chicago, Illinois.)

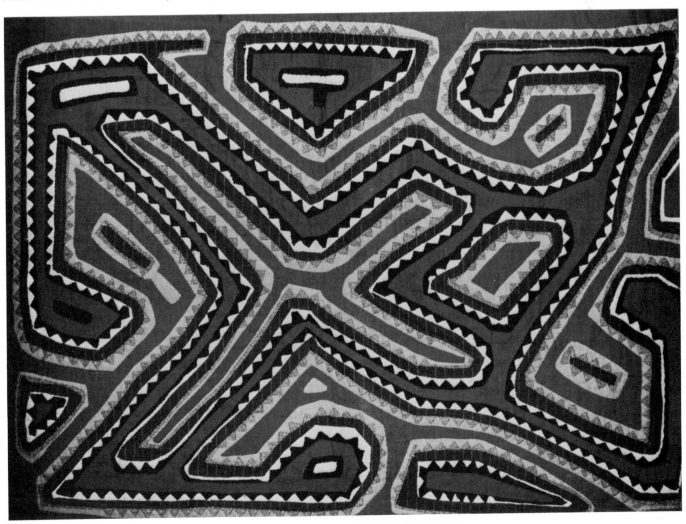

Fig. 2-13. Baby's mola with hood, made before 1919. The hood, made from a red and yellow headscarf, is unusual. (Courtesy of the Field Museum of Natural History, Chicago, Illinois.)

Fig. 2-14. A four-color mola made before 1919. The gathered piece at the bottom is a flounce. (Courtesy of the Field Museum of Natural History, Chicago, Illinois.)

The mola continued to evolve, and, by the early 1940s, the designs had become most elaborate. Not only were the Indian women making geometric patterns and depicting the flora and fauna that they saw around them, but now, with day tourists being admitted to some islands for the first time and with World War II creating more jobs for Cuna men in the Canal Zone, there was wider access to magazines, canned goods labels, cigarette packages, etc., all of which were avidly copied in molas, complete with English or Spanish decorative printing that was treated purely as design so that the letters might be altered at will to fill spaces or otherwise distorted.

At about this same time, small squares of cloth were being supplied to the women of San Blas directly from Colón rather than from the boats of the coconut traders and, while the price, as much as 5 cents for about 4 square inches, was exorbitant, this probably increased the number of available hues. Molas with four basic colors with a riot of additional shades placed under the top layer as inlay (see color plate C-1) became the most common, although some women added bits of appliqué to the upper layer instead. The spearhead of this development in the 1940s was the island of Cartí in the Gulf of San Blas where tourists visited. It has been said that in this area it was considered necessary for an Indian girl to have at least a dozen new molas in her trousseau.

For a long time, chain stitch embroidery on a panel identified it as coming from around Cartí. Usually there are just bits of embroidery done in a single strand of thread, and it is used most often to effect a change of color or for details where even a tiny appliqué would take up too much space. Sometimes, however, it is elaborate, as in color plate C-12, where multicolor spirals of chain stitch fill most of the area inside the bottle. Other decorative stitches are also found on molas, especially running stitch (color plates C-3 and C-4).

Recently I found a group of molas that were signed with various Spanish names in chain stitch. The fact that the mola was signed was no indication of the quality, which varied greatly. I bought one of these that had an excellent design but only tolerable workmanship (fig. 2-15) and have since realized that the fine, bold chain stitch in the signature was probably not done by the same person who worked the chain-stitch details in the mola itself and who had barely mastered the embroidery technique. Unfortunately, by that time, the opportunity to reexamine the others had been lost.

The mola reached its height of development in the 1950s and early 1960s. Some were made for the Indian women themselves, but others were obviously designs that were never meant to be worn on the human figure and must have been made for the tourist trade only. Very great differences between the front and back panels of a blouse appeared for the first time during this period. Although the reader will not be able to understand why before studying Chapter 4, this probably indicates that, as a result of the tourist trade, some women not only had access to larger supplies of cloth, but that they were turning out some designs almost wholesale.

Since the 1960s, molas have become better known outside Panama due to two major factors. One is the numerous exhibitions of them in galleries all over the United States and the second is the recent clamor for high fashion garments that incorporate them. The demand, in fact, has exceeded the supply and many poor molas are flooding the market.

Fig. 2-15. A signed mola, mid-1970s.

Mola-making has usually been pursued more avidly in areas visited by outsiders or where the Indians were otherwise in a position to gain money through their craft. Thus, there are some places, more remote, where the art has not advanced at all and women in out-of-the-way villages were reported in 1956 still to be wearing the original white chemise and may continue to do so still.

At Narganá, where most women have worn modern dress ever since the twenties, the youngsters are still taught to turn out molas as gifts and items for sale. Small purses are also traditional on this island.

The Cuna women who live in Colombia rather than in Panama are said to have made inferior molas, if they made them at all. Today, an American woman is teaching them to make the panels in a village where the art is said to have been lost, and has found markets for the products in New York.

Figs. 2-16 and 2-17. Mola panels from both sides of the same blouse, late 1950s or early 1960s. Very great differences between the front and back panels of a blouse appeared for the first time during this period. (Courtesy of the Field Museum of Natural History, Chicago, Illinois.)

Figs. 2-18 and 2-19. Small purses from Narganá. (Courtesy of Susan B. Black.)

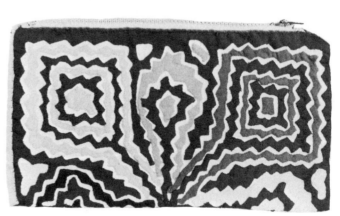

The United States Peace Corps

During the 1960s, the United States Peace Corps came to San Blas. Some of the volunteers helped organize cooperatives among the Indian women to enable them to find more profitable markets for their appliqué. Mola-decorated clothing and novelties were produced: chic women's dresses, children's clothes including small boys' overalls with decorated bibs, men's vests and neckties, bikinis, triangular headscarfs, eyeglass cases, headbands, and bags for which three-quarter-size molas were specially made. Since the Indians did not always have access to good-quality cloth, all of the materials for the project were specially purchased in Panama City. The fabrics were cut out at the cooperative headquarters and the pieces that were to become handmade mola patterns were stacked and basted together and parcelled out to women all over the Territory who had demonstrated that they could meet the standards set for the project, the ability to cut a fine design and the requirement to use matching thread. Magnificent work was turned out. The colors were not all the usual mola colors, however. The women were given a choice between those they themselves preferred and the more subdued combinations that might be more likely to appeal to the proposed market. It was decided to use some of both, although many of the Cuna color combinations did not sell readily. When the parts were finished, they were returned to the cooperative office where the garments were assembled using sewing machines. The retail outlet was another Peace Corps-sponsored cooperative in Panama City, and the project was launched with a fashion show at a debutantes' ball there. It was not only successful, but it also brought a gift of two dozen newer sewing machines to the cooperative in San Blas. Political turmoil finally resulted in expulsion of the Peace Corps from Panama, and the business no longer operates, but its activities did much to introduce the Cuna people and their handicraft into circles where they were unknown before.

A story became widespread that the Peace Corps had introduced sewing machines to San Blas and was teaching the Indians to make molas on them. This blithely ignored the fact that the project was not making molas at all, but was merely adapting the technique to a new use. Furthermore, there were hand-powered machines in the Territory at least two decades before. Are there mola panels being made on the sewing machine in San Blas? Two people, including a former Peace Corps volunteer, tell me that they have seen it being done. Let the mola buyer who wants a genuine example of the art beware.

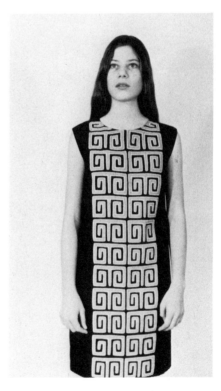

Figs. 2-20 and 2-21. Dresses made by the Peace Corps cooperative in San Blas. The dresses were assembled on the sewing machine after the mola decorations were done by hand. (Courtesy of Patricia L. Reynolds.)

Design and Characteristics of the Mola Panel

Mola panels vary greatly in size, but the average is probably about 16×19 inches. There are very small ones for babies' blouses such as that pictured in Figure 2-13 and, at the other extreme, mola skirts (figs. 2-9 and 2-10), now seldom if ever made, which are about 27 inches long. The goods most often used are fine, smooth, solid-colored cottons such as percale, but slightly coarser, more open-weave cloth is also frequently found, particularly, but not exclusively in the bottom layer. The mola technique transforms these simple materials into a new fabric that appears to have a carved surface.

When we think of molas, we think first of brilliant, intense color in all the primary hues and their complements: red, yellow, blue, green, purple, and orange. Of these, red is certainly the favorite. Black is used almost as often as red, and white also appears, but too seldom to be considered characteristic. Beyond that, it does not pay to generalize about which colors show up in molas, for one finds too many exceptions to any rule that may be set forth. However, as Chapter 4 will show more clearly, two colors or sets of colors always alternate with each other in the basic structure of a classic panel. This is more easily apparent in a linear design, but it is also true when the mola depicts an object or objects.

Fig. 2-22. An atypical linear mola. Here vertical strips of different colors were laid over the bottom layer and the top layer placed over all. (Courtesy of the Field Museum of Natural History, Chicago, Illinois.)

Fig. 2-23. Mola panel. The decorative elements may be stylized faces. (Courtesy of Lorraine D. Trebilcock.)

36

Colors are combined in molas in striking ways that would not readily occur to most of us, and often Op-art effects are produced. Very frequently, for example, a shape in one color is ringed with its complement, causing both hues to become radiantly intense because each produces an afterimage of the other. If value and intensity are just right, the result can be like a neon sign that blinks on and off. In linear designs especially, this combination of complementary colors will be spread evenly across the entire face of the panel and it will alternate with lines in which one of the colors is found by itself or in combination with something else. This produces even more afterimages of its complement. Lines of red surrounded by green, for instance, may be positioned between lines of the same red surrounded by hot pink.

Ambiguities as to what constitutes foreground and background contribute to the excitement of the mola, and spacial relationships are frequently a shifting play of planes. The following remarks apply chiefly to linear designs. In the average two-color mola, if the border is discounted, both applique and background tend to be of equal interest resulting in counterchanging effects. In most three-color panels, the eye pairs the lines of one appliqué alternately first with the lines of the other and then with those of the background to produce a kind of seesaw effect. In a pattern of four or more hues, the physical background, because comparatively little of it shows, often tends to disappear visually and the less interesting set of colors in the foreground appears to be the background. As is typical in molas, both sets of colors are spread over the entire design in such a way that they alternate with one another (see Chapter 4), and thus the space in the panel is well filled and the apparent background shapes are always as interesting as the foreground shapes. The narrow line of the true background can play many roles depending on its color. If it is one that appears to recede greatly, it may make everything else seem to float in front of it.

Fig. 2-24. Mola panel. A linear design of the early 1970s. (Courtesy of Wilma Birkeland.)

In molas that depict objects, the alternation of colors still applies to the basic structure but the lines do not cover the entire panel. Various devices are used to break up the foreground and background so that there is never a wide expanse of any one color. This may be inlay, appliqué, embroidery, or a combination of these three techniques. Shapes are often distorted in order to fit them into the available space. This is particularly apparent when a letter or numeral is stretched out or otherwise manipulated to avoid an empty spot.

The Indian woman never repeats a motif. If there are a dozen frogs or turtles on a mola, each will be differentiated from all the others in some slight design element or by being a different size. Similarly, in a bisymmetrical mola, one side of the design will be just a little different from the other, and where the pattern is symmetrical both horizontally and vertically, all four quarters will show at least some small distinctions.

Fig. 2-25. Mola panel. A popular design of which there are many variations. (Courtesy of the Field Museum of Natural History, Chicago, Illinois.)

Fig. 2-26. Mola panel. This design from the early 1970s appears to be a more modern version of the one in Figure 2-25. (Courtesy of Mrs. James C. Andrews.)

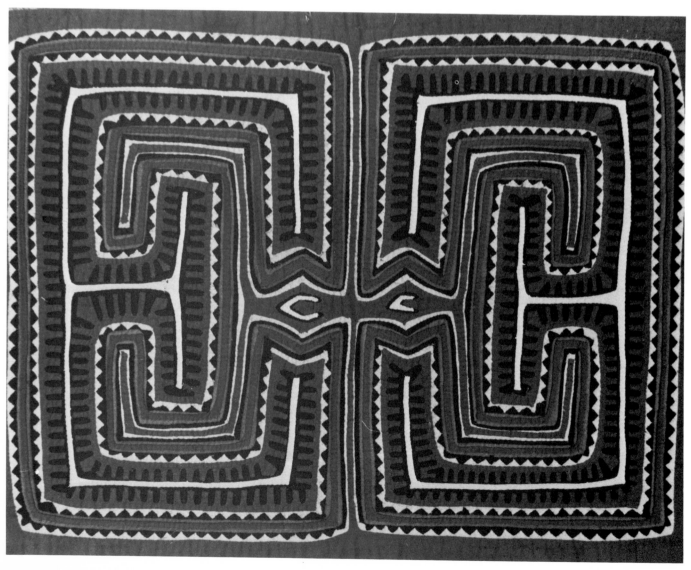

Fig. 2-27. Mola panel. Flowers and animals are favorite mola subjects. This one is unusually delicate and the little ovals look like gems in a setting. (Courtesy of the Field Museum of Natural History, Chicago, Illinois.)

Fig. 2-28. Mola panel. A design from the late 1950s or early 1960s of massed flowers with an unusual amount of embroidery. (Courtesy of the Field Museum of Natural History, Chicago, Illinois.)

Fig. 2-29. A black-and-white mola panel from the early 1970s, with wings in color. (Courtesy of Mrs. James C. Andrews.)

Fig. 2-30. Mola panel with squirrel design, early 1970s. (Courtesy of Wilma Birkeland.)

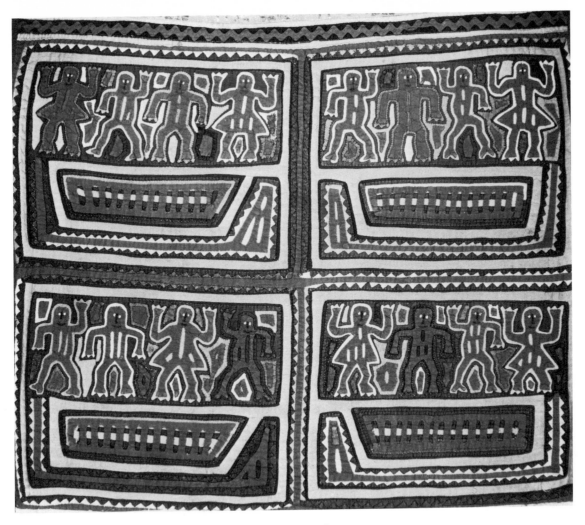

Fig. 2-31. Mola panel. This design, which appears to be men in boats, is one that comes in many versions. (Courtesy of the Field Museum of Natural History, Chicago, Illinois.)

Fig. 2-32. Mola panel, late 1950s or early 1960s. Numbers and letters are often used in molas without regard to whether they are upsidedown, backwards, or both. Featherstitches fill the eagle's wings. (Courtesy of the Field Museum of Natural History, Chicago, Illinois.)

While some mola designs are in the public domain, so to speak, others are handed down in families and are not copied by outsiders. There are styles in molas. New inventions become popular among the Indians and then give way to other ideas. Obviously innovation is admired and it is spurred on by competition. Almost anything that the Cuna woman sees or can imagine may become the subject of a mola. The list is endless—linear designs, some of which depict objects, native flora and fauna, alphabets, the Indians' own rich legends and traditions, objects from other cultures found in magazines, and advertisements including airplanes and parachutists. Some of the more startling molas are trademarks, such as RCA Victor's "His Master's Voice" or Kool Cigarettes' penguin, and cartoon characters like Bugs Bunny and Halloween witches. Molas representing Biblical themes such as the Crucifixion or the story of Adam and Eve were common for a time, though they are now rare. They produced a counter-movement in which subjects were taken from the Indian's own religion, including depictions of the soul journeying to Heaven and birth of the first snakes.

Fig. 2-33. Mola panel, late 1950s or early 1960s. (Courtesy of the Field Museum of Natural History, Chicago, Illinois.)

Fig. 2-34. Mola panel, late 1950s or early 1960s. (Courtesy of the
Field Museum of Natural History, Chicago, Illinois.)

Fig. 2-35. Mola panel, late 1950s or early 1960s. (Courtesy of
the Field Museum of Natural History, Chicago, Illinois.)

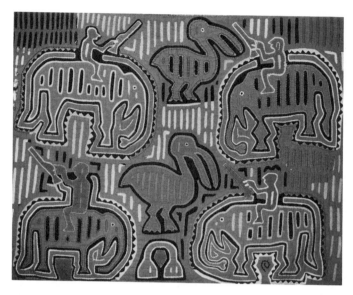

Fig. 2-36. Mola panel, late 1950s or early 1960s. (Courtesy of the Field Museum of Natural History, Chicago, Illinois.)

Fig. 2-37. Mola panel based on a political poster, late 1950s or early 1960s. (Courtesy of the Field Museum of Natural History, Chicago, Illinois.)

Fig. 2-38. Mola panel. Another version of the poster in Figure 2-37. This design is found very frequently in many variations. (Courtesy of the Field Museum of Natural History, Chicago, Illinois.)

Fig. 2-39. Mola panel. This design and the one in Figure 2-38 appear on opposite sides of the same blouse. (Courtesy of the Field Museum of Natural History, Chicago, Illinois.)

Fig. 2-40. Mola panel. Another political poster with portraits of the candidates, late 1950s or early 1960s. (Courtesy of the Field Museum of Natural History, Chicago, Illinois.)

Fig. 2-41. Mola panel, late 1950s or early 1960s. (Courtesy of the Field Museum of Natural History, Chicago, Illinois.)

Fig. 2-42. Mola panel, late 1950s or early 1960s. (Courtesy of the Field Museum of Natural History, Chicago, Illinois.)

Fig. 2-43. Mola panel, late 1950s or early 1960s. Adam and
Eve ("Adam y Eva") in the Garden. (Courtesy of the Field
Museum of Natural History, Chicago, Illinois.)

Fig. 2-44. Mola patches. Small objects like these are often made by children who are learning mola-making. (Courtesy of Lillian Brulc.)

Many Cuna women devote all their spare time to mola-making. Even so, a complete panel takes at least a month or two to complete. The Indians learn the art as children, and they are said to begin with small projects such as the miniature shown in color plate C-17 and the patches in Figure 2-44. Of course, not all women make molas and not all are equally skilled. Some sew them for other islanders at a price. The less talented woman or someone who cannot vanquish all the competition among the other women in her village may have recourse to the medicine man who, for a stiff fee, will chant over her as he anoints her eyes with a salve made from the leaves of a special tree thought to endow the recipient of these attentions with outstanding artistic talents. Although molas are normally women's province, men have sometimes cut the designs into the cloth. As the reader will realize after studying Chapter 4, a single set of cutting lines is common to all layers and after these have been indicated, the stitcher can take over, since all work in the basic structure, no matter how complicated it seems, follows logically from that point on.

Fig. 2-45. Mola headscarf. These, too, could be learning pieces for Indian girls. They are not worn by the Cuna but are sold to tourists. (Courtesy of Wilma Birkeland.)

3.

Appliqué

Appliqué is fabric design accomplished by cutting material in a decorative or expressive fashion and sewing it on top of another, usually larger, piece of cloth which contrasts in color, tone, or texture. The word was borrowed from the French and means "put on" or "applied." Sometimes holes are cut in the background fabric, or matrix, and the decorative fragments sewn on underneath so that they show through. Nowadays, this too, is often called appliqué, but, strictly speaking, it is the easiest form of *inlay*, and it will simplify our discussion of molas if we are careful to make the distinction. There are several ways to do appliqué. This chapter includes not only the methods best suited to molas and reverse appliqué (see Chapter 5) but it also tries to show beginners the easiest approach to a fascinating skill. Hopefully, the overview will encourage mixtures of techniques that perhaps

craftsmen have not considered before.

In either appliqué or inlay, when the applied cloth is pasted or merely tacked down rather than sewn on, the work then becomes *collage*, from a French word meaning "to paste" or "to glue." Appliqué is suitable for clothing, quilts, wall-hangings, stuffed toys, pillows, boxes and many other objects. Do not use it where it will receive much rubbing. Chair seats and piano bench covers, for instance, should be worked in a sturdier technique that uses long-wearing materials, such as crewel or needlepoint, if they are to last any reasonable amount of time at all.

Fig. 3-1. *Left:* partially-completed appliqué sample. *Right:* inlay. In appliqué, a design is cut out, placed over another piece of cloth, and sewn down. In inlay, holes are cut in the background fabric and a contrasting piece is slipped underneath.

Equipment

The necessary equipment for the appliqué techniques, including reverse appliqué and inlay, is simple and inexpensive (fig. 3-2). It can be purchased locally, the sewing gear at fabric stores and the other items at stationers or art supply stores. Usually, it is already on hand in homes where people like to stitch. The bare minimum needs are needles and thread in assorted colors, rustproof straight pins, embroidery scissors to snip with, shears for cutting cloth, and perhaps a pencil.

Everything else is optional depending on the sort of work planned and the methods used. We have given fairly complete lists, though most beginners will want to pick and choose as they experiment with one type of work or another.

Wooden toothpicks speed things up in hand sewing when used for pushing under seam allowances. They do a better job than just the needle you are working with. Flat ones are preferable, though round ones are helpful also. Discard them when they wear smooth and no longer drag the fabric under.

An *iron* can be used to press under seam allowances on small or uncomplicated appliqués. This, too, makes for speed. Iron and board are generally needed for final pressing and when sewing garments.

Those who want to bond their materials together instead of sewing them will find that, in addition to the special *glues* made for cloth, excellent *fabric adhesives* that are applied with an iron are available. Polyamide, which is the chemical constituent of these different products, is washable and drycleanable, and can be used to bond fabrics to cardboard, metal, and wood as well as to each other. Be sure to read and follow the directions. Newer products, like a spray that holds patterns to cloth without pinning are fun to try, but can add considerably to the expense. Investigate them at your fabric store if they interest you.

The *sewing machine* is popular with many for doing applique, and even those who put their decorative patches on by hand sometimes find it useful for transferring designs to fabric. Machine embroidery and appliqué make an excellent pair. An eight-inch embroidery hoop is usually needed for this. You do not have to buy the special

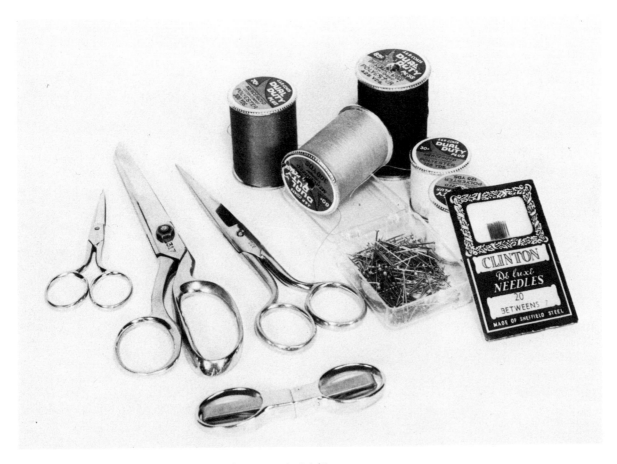

Fig. 3-2. Appliqué requires scissors with which to cut cloth (either of the larger pair) a pair of small, sharp, pointed scissors for snipping, needles, pins, and thread in assorted colors. Everything else is optional. The 6-inch embroidery scissors is the first pair to the left of the thread.

kind carried where machines are sold if you look for metal or wooden ones thin enough to slip under a presser foot when turned sideways, but some of the newer plastic hoops are much too thick. A book on machine embroidery by Jennifer Gray is listed in the Bibliography.

For drawing designs, assemble *drawing tools* such as: no. 2 and other pencils, felt-tipped pens, crayons, paints, rulers, compasses, French curves, circular objects and other shapes to trace around, artists' tracing paper, tissue paper, brown wrapping paper, colored construction paper and the like to draw on or cut shapes from.

For transferring design to fabric various *cutting* and *tracing equipment* is necessary such as: dressmakers' or other nonsmudging carbon paper and tracing wheel (or sharp-pointed stick or metal stylus), scissors for cutting paper (never use the same scissors you use for cutting fabric), transparent tape (preferably the kind you can write on), double-faced transparent tape, white glue, stapler.

Templates can be helpful when working with many small, simple, identical pieces as in some quilt-making. Cut them in light cardboard if the edges are to be folded over with an iron, but if they are to be patterns for cutting only, add the seam allowances to the templates and use sandpaper or some other material that will not slide on the fabric as you trace around the shape with a pencil. A large bulletin board is very convenient for laying paper or cloth cutouts directly onto the background fabric and judging the results from a distance, but a dressmaker's dummy is a better choice for those who are primarily interested in making clothing.

To embellish applied work, collect *stitchery equipment* such as embroidery needles, embroidery thread, yarn, and string of all sorts, found objects such as beads, bells, *shisha* glass, shells, and bits of braid, ribbon, lace, and so forth. Embroidery hoops may be used for the decorative work, but do not try to do the appliqué itself on a background stretched in such a frame. The result will not be

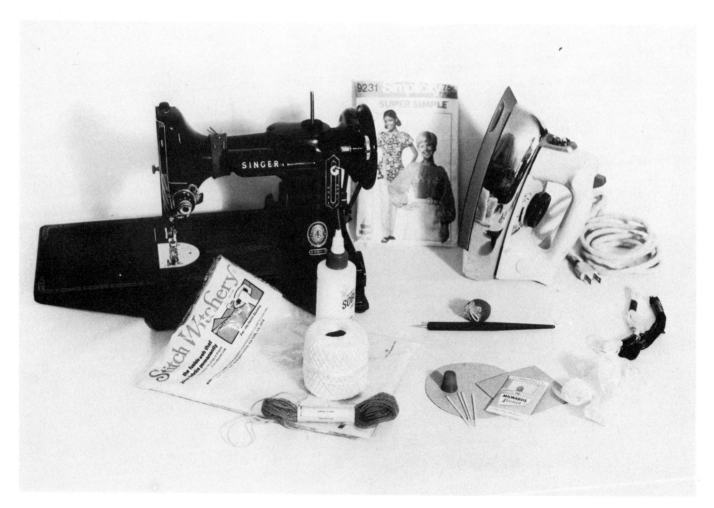

Fig. 3-3. Only a small selection of the sewing and embroidery equipment that might be used in appliqué depending on the individual needs of the worker. In the center are an emery ball and a stylus. The stylus is ordinarily used for making drawings on mimeograph stencils. It is somewhat more satisfactory than a tracing wheel when working with dressmaker's carbon paper in embroidery and appliqué, and it can be purchased in stationery stores. Cardboard templates are under the needles and the thimble. The lace at lower right represents trimmings and found objects of all sorts.

satisfactory, because appliqué and background cannot both be stretched with equal tension. You can, however, mount the background *permanently* on artists' stretchers before beginning hand appliqué work, and for this you will also need a staple gun. Incidentally, for more body, mount a piece of thin muslin first underneath the background. Do not forget that you can apply bits of your own weaving, crocheting, tatting, or other handwork for added interest and texture.

For padded appliqué, various *fillings* are required. Try layers of felt. Cotton and dacron batting or stuffing are also good choices as are worn, snipped, nylon stockings.

Those who are putting their appliqué on clothing may need *commercial patterns*.

Those who are using their appliqué decoratively will need *mounting equipment and tools:* wood, metal, or other material for armatures, and wooden dowels or other means of suspension for wall hangings. To work with heavy leather, you may need an awl or a special needle.

These can usually be bought where you buy your leather. Curved needles are useful for those who make boxes.

If *blocking equipment* is necessary to finish work that has puckered, a piece of fiber insulation board such as Celotex, which can be purchased at lumber yards, may be used as a blocking board. After marking it in squares with a pencil, cover it with a piece of plastic painter's dropcloth (the thinnest, cheapest variety) and stretch your work on it using heavy rustproof pins and a thimble. Small things can be stretched with pins on slabs of Styrofoam (plastic foam) to which has been pinned graph paper covered with ordinary clear plastic wrap. (You must cover graph paper with the wrap or the ink will run onto your work.)

Other *finishing equipment* that might be wanted includes sprays that protect fabric from dust and moisture, starch or fabric finish, and acrylic spray.

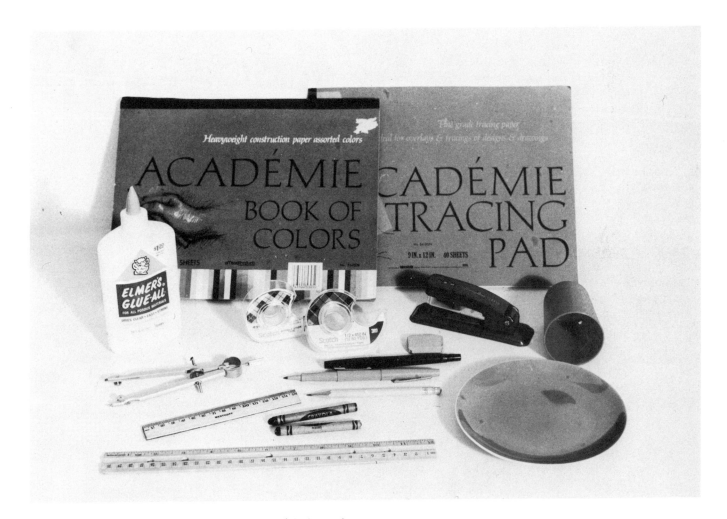

Fig. 3-4. A small sampling of the equipment that might be used for making appliqué designs. Only the tracing paper and the pencil are at all essential, and some people choose to do without them. The cup and plate are to trace around to make circles and ovals.

Sewing Hints

Without adequate scissors, only very crude appliqué work can be achieved. To turn back a curved cloth edge, you must be able to snip the seam allowances neatly and accurately. For this you need straight, sharp embroidery scissors which are about three inches long (fig. 3-2). Small folding scissors (shown at lower center) came on the market a few years ago and are adequate if they are of good quality. Many people try to use cuticle scissors with curved blades but these are not at all suitable even when very sharp and strong, which they seldom are. Then, because small snipping scissors do not cut cloth smoothly, but tend to hack it into jagged pieces, a larger pair is needed also. These can be your dressmaker shears if you have them, but, if you often cut out fairly small pieces of cloth, six-inch embroidery scissors (shown next to the pins) are much more convenient. Both pairs of scissors should be of good enough quality to be worth sharpening when necessary, a service that can often be obtained at hardware stores. If scissors are used only for cutting cloth and snipping thread, they will generally stay sharp for years and years.

For fine hand sewing, the needles called *betweens*, which are shorter than the more commonly used *sharps*, are the best choice. Size 7 is an appropriate size for work with ordinary sewing thread. They can be found in fabric stores and wherever more than just a token supply of needles is stocked. Never work with a darning needle since they are designed to be extra-long, which facilitates the weaving that is done when darning but makes the needles too clumsy for ordinary sewing. Mercerized cotton-covered polyester thread is excellent for hand sewing since it twists and frays very little. The 100% polyester thread does not pull through fabric smoothly and is not at all relaxing to work with when sewing by hand. Save it for your machine sewing. Use pins that will not leave large holes in your work. Silk pins are best for the lightweight fabrics used in most appliqué, but it is convenient to have somewhat heavier ones on hand, too. These should also be good quality rustproof dressmaker pins.

If the hand stitching in appliqué is to be invisible, it must be done with a single thread, not a double one (fig. 3-5). If you failed to learn this technique as a child, try it again now, using the proper needle to help keep the thread from pulling out. With ordinary sewing cotton, this is size 7. If you still can't do it, try knotting the thread into the eye of the needle as shown in Figure 3-6. Tie a single knot only as shown in the diagram and pull tight. The knot won't interfere with your sewing, but it does have to be cut each time you come to the end of your thread. If you have trouble threading your needle and can't keep track of your needle threader, try this same trick using a fine crewel needle. Don't use a large crewel needle that leaves holes in the fabric, though. There are also needles for easy threading that are open at the top of the eye except for a tiny spring, but even the smallest ones do not pull through the cloth as smoothly as regular needles, and the knot trick is better. Incidentally, a needle that is too small may bend, break, or get caught in the fabric at the eye. It will not make a big enough hole, and your thread will fray as it is pulled through the cloth.

Fig. 3-6. Knotting the thread into the eye of the needle.

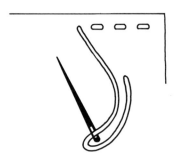

Fig. 3-5. Sewing with a single rather than with a double thread.

Two sewing accessories that are neglected today are emery balls for sharpening pins and needles and thimbles. Emery balls usually come as tiny red strawberry pincushions attached to the larger tomato-shaped pincushions that can be bought at most notions counters. Pushing your needle rapidly through an emery ball several times will sharpen it, clean it, remove rust, and make it easier to work with on hot, sticky days. I was told as a child never to use an emery ball for a pincushion because the needles left in it would rust. Never having had occasion to break the rule, I don't know if this is true or not.

Thimbles take a little getting used to but they make stitching so much faster and more comfortable that it is well worth the trouble. Perhaps people misunderstand and think they should push the needle with the top of the thimble, an almost impossible feat when using a standard-length needle. Certainly there are useless thimbles to be found that have smooth sides and indentations on the top only. Actually, you wear it on the middle finger of your right hand (get one that fits comfortably) and push the eye end of the needle with the side of the thimble as you take each stitch (fig. 3-7). Practice for only a few minutes each time you sit down to sew. You will soon find you cannot do without this tool, for it not only pushes the needle through difficult places without making your finger sore, but it also eliminates all the pulling and tugging that many people do and helps you to go faster even when only sewing two light layers together. You will probably find that using a between needle makes it easier to learn to work with a thimble.

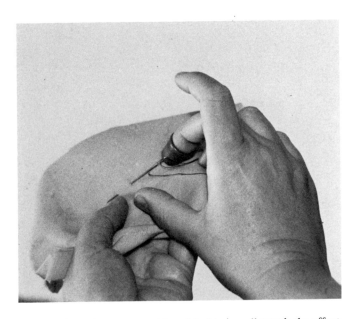

Fig. 3-7. Learning to sew with a thimble is well worth the effort. As you take a stitch, push with the side of the thimble, not the top, for that would be a difficult feat. Here thumb and forefinger have been held aside to show this movement, and an extra-long needle has been used.

Fabrics

Appliqué is centuries old and, over the years, plain and printed fabric made of all sorts of fibers woven in almost every way has been used: silk, wool, linen, cotton, synthetics, blends, muslins, twills, velvets, brocades, transparent gauzes, and so forth. Even nonwoven materials like leather and felt are popular, and knits and plastics are now being used also.

Success in applying cloth depends largely on whether you select the right technique for the fabric you want to use, or the right fabric for the technique if you are working in a classic form and do not mean to deviate from the traditional method. What the object being made will be used for and whether or not it will have to be washed or dry cleaned must also be considered. Do not forget to preshrink everything that needs it, and avoid the use of fabrics that are not dye-fast when they ought to be. Knowing what to do in any particular case is largely a matter of experience, but here are some guidelines.

The most versatile fabrics are fairly lightweight, smooth, opaque, closely woven so that they fray little, and have little give or stretch. Percale and cotton broadcloth fall into this category and come in a wide range of solid colors. They can be handled in almost any of the ways discussed here, but their chief virtues are that their edges can be turned under and hemmed down invisibly without the need for further embellishment, and that fairly complicated outlines are possible as in molas and Hawaiian quilts. Today, however, special finishes and fiber blends are common in almost all yard goods, and fabrics that appear to be cotton may have large admixtures of man-made fibers. The beginner, therefore, having found something that appears to be suitable will do well to apply a simple test: fold over a narrow hem at the cut edge of the material and crease it heavily with your fingers. If the fabric pops back up it will be much harder to work with than it will be if it stays down. Materials like organdy that have the same attributes as the above, except that they are not opaque, can often be hemmed if the shapes are simple and the turnings kept narrow and even. However, they are more often applied flat in traditional work with couched cord, punchwork or other embroidery used to camouflage the raw edges, as described in the following section. In contemporary work, multiple layers of net and other transparents are often used to effect changes in color.

Stretchy knits and delicate or loosely-woven fabrics may be stabilized before using them for appliqué by bonding them to a thin backing. This technique was used in the past to preserve worn bits of precious fabric. Ordinary flour paste was used then, but today we have excellent bonding materials such as polyamide and other fabric glues. Whenever ironing a knit or other highly textured fabric, place it face down on several thicknesses of turkish toweling. If you want to apply a white or light-colored fabric to a very dark background, but the patch is not quite opaque enough to hide the dark color, bond it to a thin piece of muslin. Bonding can also be used for closely-woven fabrics to make it unnecessary to turn under or cover the edges, but do not expect to sew down anything bonded to a *nonwoven* fabric by taking tiny stitches over the edge. The stitches will not hold and the patch will tend to disintegrate. Gauzy or transparent materials cannot be bonded.

Fabrics that are hard to appliqué because they fray easily or for some other reason may be inlaid in a more tractable material so that it is the easier-to-handle cloth that is turned under and sewn (see fig. 3-1). Do not trim the difficult fabric too close to the stitching. Such pieces can also be bound or laid on in such a way that all the raw edges are overlapped by other, sturdier patches or are covered with heavy embroidery.

Very bulky fabrics cannot usually be applied to very delicate ones without causing undesirable puckering or buckling. Felts and leathers need no turnings and are easily sewn on with handsome results, though felt has a tendency to fade, and soft leathers might be cut by stitching too tightly with fine thread. Heavy leather may have to have holes bored in it with an awl before it can be stitched. Fabric can be smocked, pleated or otherwise folded, gathered, or manipulated before being used as appliqué. Needlepoint can be applied by inlaying it or by other methods described in books on needlepoint.

It is impossible to make specific recommendations about which fabrics ought to be used for appliqué foundations when the materials that can be applied to them are almost limitless, as are the techniques for applying them, and when readers will want to make everything from clothing to sculpture and stuffed toys. Obviously the fabric has to be firm and sturdy enough to support the appliqués, and obviously it must be easy to stitch through. A lining for the backing material of inexpensive fabric like batiste or unbleached muslin (the two layers are then stitched through as though they were one fabric) will lend richness, especially if the object is to hang or drape, but this is not always necessary. Sometimes it is inadvisable, if, for example, the backing fabric is transparent or a double fabric is too heavy. Occasionally it may be worthwhile to line the backing only behind the appliqués and then cut away the excess lining after they are sewn down. This is an area where little advice can be given, lacking specific information, but here are some things that may inspire imaginative projects.

Piece three to five kinds of cloth that are different in color or texture into a well-proportioned and harmonious background, and play off the appliqué against it in contrapuntal fashion (see fig. 3-8).

Try a backing fabric that has a fairly open even weave, like homespun or burlap, that can be textured with counted-thread embroidery in the places where it is left bare of appliqué. Some pulled fabric stitches are effective when worked in fine crewel wool on burlap, but remember that *colored* burlap has a tendency to fade badly.

Put appliqué both above and below transparent backings, perhaps for double-faced effects, such as room-dividers that can be seen from both sides.

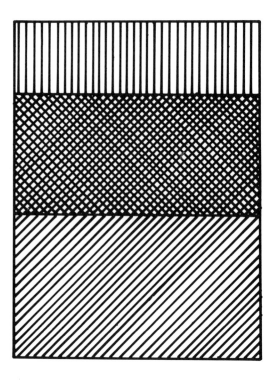

Fig. 3-8. Piece three to five kinds of cloth that are different in color or texture into a well-proportioned background and play off the appliqué against it in a contrapuntal fashion. This is only one possible arrangement.

Basic Techniques
Appliqué

Appliqué offers so much variety that it has something for almost everybody. It can be done by hand or on the sewing machine. Sometimes, after the patches are laid flat on the background, their raw edges are covered with embroidery. More often, the cutouts are hemmed and sewn down as invisibly as possible, in order to play off shape against shape or fabric against fabric without the visual interference of bold or even obvious stitchery.

Beginners might start by sampling the various methods to see which they prefer. Begin with cotton scraps for patches, although it is probably better for people who are not used to manipulating fabric to avoid permanent press or durable press fabrics at first since they tend to puff up and the edges do not crease easily for turning under.

In the early stages, it is more interesting to change the background, or at least its color, for each new motif that you sew down. Use a series of seven- or eight-inch foundation squares instead of a single large piece of cloth. If you like, the smaller squares can be sewn together after the appliqué is finished to make a pillow, a wallhanging, or a handbag. Denim makes an especially good background, but percale, broadcloth, and similar fabrics can also be used. Do not forget to preshrink appliqué fabric, backing, linings, and trimmings. *Selvages*, the quarter-inch or so at each side of the material which is woven more densely than the body of the fabric, should be cut off and discarded from just the piece you are using. Do not cut it off anything else for the moment.

For designs, choose simple shapes that are at least 3 inches across. Make them, for the time being, by tracing directly on the face of the fabric with a pencil around glasses, French curves, large cookie cutters and the like, and using a ruler to draw squares and rectangles. Try to include an example of each technical item discussed below, but do not follow the models slavishly.

First, learn the few easy tricks for turning under the hems of cutout shapes. Begin with a simple square or rectangle and learn to miter corners. Draw the shape directly on the right side of your appliqué fabric with a pencil. This line is the *seamline* where the cloth will be creased and turned under. Most people find it easier to work with a clearly-delineated seamline. This may be a mark made with a pencil or a sheet of non-smudge or dressmakers' carbon paper, but, after the preliminary exercises, it is preferable to use a row of hand or machine stitching or a crease made with an iron. These are all ways of marking that do not show when the work is finished. The marks are generally put in when transferring the design to the fabric. There is seldom need to mark the background material.

Next, pencil in your *cutting line*, as shown by the interrupted lines in Figure 3-9. For the time being, this should be a consistent ¼-inch away from the seamline. As you become more expert, you will probably prefer to cut out your appliqué directly without drawing in this line first. The area between the seamline and the cutting line is the *seam allowance*. You will soon find that you want to make it only about ⅛-inch wide when using fine materials like percale, and that you will need to widen it when handling difficult fabrics that fray easily.

Having cut out the rectangle or square along the cutting line, you can proceed in one of two ways. You can use an iron, in which case you lay the patch wrong-side-up on the board and press back each corner as shown by the diagonal solid line at the lower left in Figure 3-9. Make sure the folds touch the intersection of the seam lines but do not go beyond it into the square itself. Next, snip away the excess fabric by cutting off the corner along the dotted line which is halfway across the seam allowance at the corner. When all 4 corners have been mitered with the iron, keep 2 of them folded and turn back the hem along the seamline between them and press it down. Repeat with the other 3 seamlines. If you are planning to handle the appliqué a good deal, moving it and others around on a background to find the most effective arrangement, for instance, it would be wise to baste the hems at this point. But, for now, it will be sufficient to lay the shape in position on its foundation and pin it down, right side up, with the hems turned under. Don't spare the pins and work from the center out, making sure that there are no puckers.

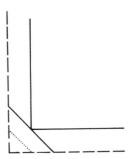

Fig. 3-9. Mitering the corners of a rectangle or square.

To work without an iron, pin the flat appliqué to the background material in the position desired, keeping it face up. Again use plenty of pins and work from the center out, making sure that there are no puckers. Keep the pins ⅜-inch inside the seamline so that they will not have to be moved when turning the hems under. Miter two adjacent corners using the same technique described in the last paragraph, but this time you will be turning them under and making the creases with your thumb. Keeping the miters in place, fold under the side between them and pin it down to the background fabric. When the second corner is reached, miter the corner that will be sewn down next, and turn under and pin the hem along the edge that precedes it. Continue in this way until the entire edge is turned and pinned. Only when the side of the appliqué is absolutely straight and the seam allowance at least ¼-inch wide, is it advisable to turn down a whole side at one time like this. Ordinarily, it is necessary to push under a little of the hem with the aid of a toothpick or the needle. The short length that is turned under is kept in position with the left thumb until the stitching is completed.

To sew invisibly by hand, use thread that matches the patch rather than the background. Secure it by taking two or three tiny back stitches over each other on the background material near where you intend to start sewing. This must be under the appliqué where the back stitches will be hidden after the hem is turned under and stitched down. When the patch has been sewn completely, finish off your thread in the same way, first taking it through to the back of the work. Stitch as shown in Figure 3-10. Hold the appliqué down with your left thumb, close to where the needle will surface, and bring the needle up on the patch as close to its edge as you can. Then, repeating a single motion until the whole patch is sewn down, insert the needle first in the background fabric immediately opposite the place where it came up and as close to the appliqué as possible, and then bring it up again about an ⅛-inch to the left, taking it through the appliqué again as close to the edge as possible.

Points are folded, trimmed and sewn exactly like mitered corners except that the seam allowance will probably have to be tapered by trimming away a little extra fabric as indicated by the dotted lines in Figure 3-11.

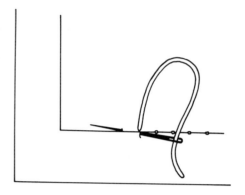

Fig. 3-10. Hemming down the appliqué.

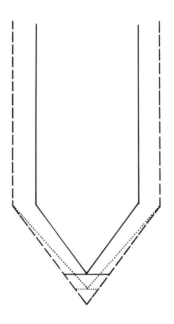

Fig. 3-11. Sewing points.

It is impossible to turn under the edges of shapes with angular corners (fig. 3-12) or curves (fig. 3-13) without clipping the seam allowances as shown in the diagrams. The cuts are made from the edge of the fabric right up to but not through the seamline. Anything more or less will distort the shape. How far apart to make them depends on the sharpness of the curve, and experience will soon show you how to clip to get the smoothest edge to your patch. To begin, keep the cuts slightly less than a ½-inch apart. Inward curves like the one on the right side of the crescent are snipped to allow the seam allowance to spread. Outward curves like the one on the left side of the crescent must be notched to remove excess fabric. Actually, though, when using material that is not bulky, it is often sufficient, and certainly much easier, to make straight snips here also and allow the excess fabric to overlap.

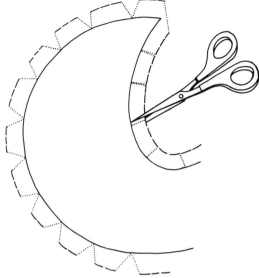

Fig. 3-13. Snipping concave and convex curves.

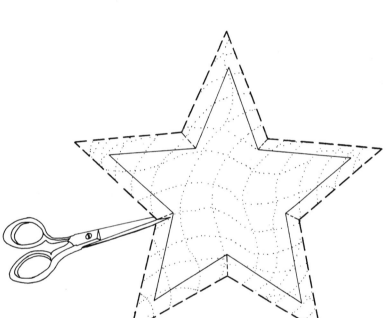

Fig. 3-12. Snipping angular corners.

To apply patches with the sewing machine, trace the seamline on the face of the fabric to be used for the appliqué as before. Cut out the appliqué, leaving the seam allowance on. This should be at least ¼-inch wide. Whether or not you need to baste after you pin it to the background depends on how carefully you pin and your skill with the machine. Sew around the shape on the seamline with an ordinary machine stitch, and then trim away the excess fabric close to the stitching but not so close that the appliqué can pull away from the stitches. Finish by covering both the stitching and the raw edge with a satin stitch (a close zigzag stitch), but omit this step if the satin-stitch edge will interfere with other hand or machine finishing such as the sewing on of braid. The thread used for the zigzagging can match or contrast with the color of the appliqué. If it matches the background, it will only serve to reduce the apparent size of the patch when the piece is viewed from a distance. The design marked on the fabric is always sewn over when the machine is used, and therefore, a pencil line is quite adequate.

Hand or machine appliqué may be stuffed by interrupting the sewing when all but about 1 inch of the patch has been sewn down onto the background, and then pushing a filling through the opening. The opening is then closed by completing the sewing. Be careful not to stretch the shape while stuffing or to distort it in sewing the final inch. Make sure the appliqué is sewn down exactly where it would have been had it not been stuffed. A row of basting may be made on the background fabric before beginning the filling process to insure this. Do not leave the opening where the sewing is more difficult than elsewhere on the shape. A crescent, for instance, should be stuffed from the middle of either side rather than at a point. If a large shape is stuffed, it may require quilting or other stitching across the area to keep the filling from shifting.

To use felt or batting for padding, tack it firmly to the background before covering it with the appliqué unless it will be caught down in the sewing. That will keep it from shifting and lumping up. If more than one layer is used, trim each one so that it is slightly smaller than the one above it. This gives a more rounded shape to the edge.

Fabric collage, or bonding or gluing of patches onto the background, is acceptable when the work will not get much handling or cleaning, but even a very careful job won't insure that the appliqué will not fray, and so, the method should be used with judgment. It might be suitable when large amounts of stitchery are to be worked freely over the surface once the appliqué is in place, or it might be used for pieces that will have a short life like banners that are to be used on only one or two occasions.

Inlay

So far we have been discussing patches that are laid on top of a background and fastened down. Inlay does not follow that rule. Originally, it consisted of cutting a shape out of the background fabric and replacing it with an identical piece in a contrasting material. This complex form of inlay, found in old British embroideries, could be done in various ways depending on what kind of cloth was being used. Often the final step was to outline the shape with cord for strength and also to cover up the cuts. Nowadays this work exists only in simplified form, at least in the United States. The shape is cut in the background fabric leaving a seam allowance, and a patch slightly larger than the hole is laid underneath (fig. 3-1), although, conceivably, the inlay could underlie the entire piece and function as a lining. The seam allowance on the *upper piece* is then clipped, turned under, and hemmed down onto the *lower piece*, using the techniques described above. Often, fabrics that are too loosely woven or too delicate to be appliquéd can be laid underneath in this way.

Stitchery

By far the most effective form of appliqué is the simplest. Good, bold design carried out in mostly solid-colored fabric, with no stitching apparent, enhances the value of the inexpensive cottons usually used for it a hundred times over. Moreover, this type of design can be distinguished from a long distance away, making it extremely effective where it will be viewed from across a large room such as a church sanctuary or a lobby. To combine stitchery with appliqué, therefore, is in some ways to gild the lily. But many people like gilded lilies, and it must be said in all fairness that much of the contemporary work that blends the two techniques is successful in a way that creates a third distinct art form from the two techniques.

Embroidery can be added to appliqué in any of several ways. It can emphasize the contours of the shapes by delineating them with contrasting thread. The embroidery in some cases is even the means by which the patches are sewn down. Almost any stitch or combination of stitches can be used, including the time-honored blanket stitch. If the spokes of the blanket-stitch point outward instead of inward, the embroidery has more visual effect on the bold appliqué shapes, creating a special feathered effect with the straight stitches pointing out and the connecting stitches forming one continuous line. Close buttonhole stitch shows up somewhat better, but is tedious to do and easily duplicated by close machine zigzagging. Chain stitch, feather stitch, and various sorts of couching are all popular and effective.

Stitchery can bring out details that are too fine for appliqué—anything from facial features to lines of stitching used to extend points into very long, narrow lines. It can be used to obscure parts of the shape or outline or for texturing. Sometimes it is worked freely over the surface of the object independent of the appliqués. Nets and other transparent fabrics are often used in conjunction with the embroidery to bring about changes in color or texture.

Transparent materials lend themselves to special handling. A double layer of organdy or some other sheer fabric is quite different in appearance from a single layer of the same fabric. Thus, in traditional work, we have lingerie and table linens that exploit this self-appliqué idea to produce fabric with, at its best, an appearance similar to Steuben or Swedish glass. Usually the patch, complete with a wide seam allowance, is laid underneath rather than on top of the background. The patch forms the doubled layer, and no hole is cut. A shiny cloth like satin can be used instead of self-fabric for the appliqué to intensify the effect. Sometimes the patch is carefully stuck to the underside of the fabric before sewing with a thin layer of transparent paste to prevent bubbles. Then the two layers are stitched together decoratively along the outlines of the shape after which the seam allowance is trimmed away. The sewing, done on the face of the work, may be satin stitch worked over a padding of cord, which can be done more easily on the sewing machine, or a type of punchwork. Punchwork consists of drawn fabric stitches worked on a diaphanous fabric where the threads are too fine to be counted. Formerly, a special needle could be bought for this, but any coarse needle will work. Use it with fine thread that matches the fabric and take tiny stitches and pull them tight so that only a pattern of holes can be seen. Figures 3-14 and 3-15 show three-sided stitch, one of the most popular patterns in punchwork. The technique demands a gauzy material and will not work with closely-woven fabrics like broadcloth.

When using a background fabric suitable for drawn thread work, square or oblong appliqués with the edges basted under may be sewn down by using hemstitching techniques.

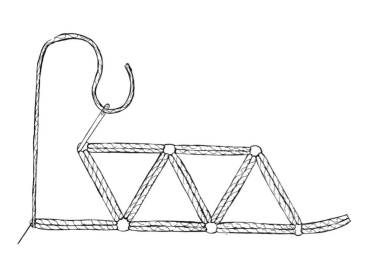

Fig. 3-14. Doing three-sided stitch.

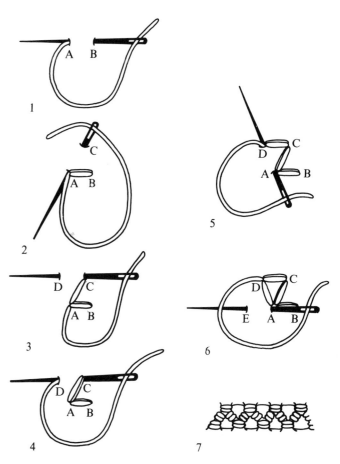

Fig. 3-15. Three-sided stitch showing the stitches pulled tight.

Fabric Grain

The beginner who has been trying out these suggestions is probably by now at least somewhat aware of fabric grain, the warp and weft of woven cloth. If nothing more, he or she may have noticed that ordinary fabric gives or stretches when pulled on the diagonal or *bias* but not otherwise and that appliqués look best when the threads of the patches are lined up with the threads of the fabric, especially if the weave is at all prominent. Structurally, this is the soundest method, particularly when the lengthwise, or warp, threads, which are the strongest and form the backbone of the weaving, run in the same direction. Much puckering can be avoided by following this rule. (When a piece of cloth, as purchased, is held up with the lengthwise grain running up and down, the cut edges of the material will be at the top and bottom and the selvages at the sides.) But matching grain can be overdone. For if the rule were never broken, you could not run stripes diagonally unless they were printed that way on the fabric, nor could you exploit the color changes that are made possible by turning some materials, satin, for instance, in different directions. Generally, small patches will cause almost no trouble in this regard, but, if puckers or bubbles threaten to appear, or when applying a large piece without regard to the grain, you may need to bond the appliqué to a light backing to nullify the effects of mismatching the fabric structure.

Pile fabrics also change color when turned in different directions, and, unless you deliberately want to exploit this fact, all pieces cut from them should lie the same way—the one that shows them to their best advantage. These materials include velveteen, corduroy, fake fur, and suede cloth. Leather is not woven, but it has a visual grain, and patterns for all pieces for the same object should be laid either crosswise or lengthwise on it as a general rule.

Unless embroidery has been worked too tightly across the surface of a piece, it is usually fabric grain that is involved when objects like skirts, wall hangings, banners, or items with many layers like reverse appliqué, pull out of shape and do not lie flat. Small amounts of buckling or puckering can often be corrected by blocking the finished product, but it is simpler and surer to make the fabric as grain perfect as you can to begin with. Wherever possible, the lengthwise grain, or warp, should be perpendicular to the floor.

Normally, the warp and weft threads in any given piece of cloth should cross each other at right angles, but, nowadays, almost all commercial fabrics are subjected to various finishing processes which pull them out of line. Most can be straightened, with the notable exception of permanent-press or durable-press fabrics. Use these as is, since the process locks the threads in position and they will pull back into their original orientation even if you should succeed in temporarily straightening the grain.

To determine whether a piece of fabric is off-grain, you must begin by straightening both raw ends. They are already straight if you can pull away the end weft or cross thread from selvage to selvage. Otherwise, in order to straighten the ends, clip the selvage and tear the fabric across if this is possible, or, if not, cut along a prominent rib, or pull out a thread and cut along it. Fold the fabric in half lengthwise. It is probably easiest for beginners to baste the edges together all around. Then, if the fabric lies flat when laid on a table, the grain is straight. If not, it can sometimes be corrected by merely pulling out on the corners of the short diagonal or by pressing with a steam iron. Difficult washable fabrics can be soaked for 15 minutes and then ironed carefully after partial drying. Let the damp fabric sit in a plastic bag for a while until the moisture has spread evenly.

With materials where the finish does not permit them to be straightened by making both warp and weft run perpendicular, choose one side to go up and down and then cut the other at a right-angle (90°) to it. In a woven fabric let the warp threads run straight up and down if you can and then cut the ends square to them. Placing the fabric on a long counter in kitchen or bathroom so that there is a straight edge to use as a guide is an enormous help. Knit fabrics do not have grain, but should be used in such a way that the lengthwise ribs are straight, unless there is a reason to do otherwise. Be careful to place these ribs straight when bonding a knit to keep it from stretching.

Two Ways of Working, with Some Notes on Design
Making Paper Cutouts

Large, bold, simple shapes are usually considered to be the best for appliqué. This concept blithely ignores the fact that some of the most admired forms of the art, notably the Hawaiian quilt and the true mola, are not designed that way. However, it is good advice for beginners who must learn to express ideas in terms of outline shapes that do not admit of much detail except as afterthoughts. A good first project begins with tacking a backing up on a large bulletin board, although some people may prefer instead to mount the backing permanently on artists' stretchers with a staple gun, or, if working with clothing, to use a dressmaker's dummy. Geometric and freeform shapes, each in a variety of sizes and colors, are then cut in cloth and moved around on the backing until a satisfactory composition is found. Use textured fabrics and prints as well as solid colors in your first project. Tack with as few pins as possible, or, if using stretchers, use a double-faced transparent tape, which is preferable. If the pieces are to be hemmed, cut patterns in several sizes for each shape out of light cardboard. Then cut several appliqués leaving seam allowances and work with an iron, clipping and pressing the edges down over the cardboard shape. Remove the cardboard and baste the hems of the patch.

Thus, you can start with a few appliqués and, as your ideas change, you can quickly make new ones in different sizes or colors to move around with or replace the first ones. Some people play with paper cutouts of various kinds, but beginners should work with the cloth itself wherever possible, for a kind of translation is necessary when replacing the paper with cloth. Anyway, using fabric is more fun, and the material as well as the shapes will suggest ideas. Be sure to evaluate your work from a distance as well as close up. Once you have a composition that satisfies you, a little pinning makes the appliqués all ready to sew. Be sure to remove any double-faced tape that you use. It is possible that, with time, it may come through and ruin the face of your panel.

If you wish, this simple, direct method can later become the basis of a more systematic study of design. Begin with smooth, solid-color fabrics with minimum textural interest and tack up your shapes as before. When you stand well away from the board, notice how a very bright color can overpower another color cut in the same size and shape and similarly positioned, how some colors seem to come forward and some to recede, and how some hues seem to vibrate when placed next to each other.

Do not sew down your composition when you are satisfied with it. Instead, gradually replace some of the elements with textured fabrics and again stand back and see what special effects they produce. Shiny white satin seems to come forward, for instance, some textures seem to be incompatible with each other, but transparent fabrics or nets can often reconcile unrelated areas when placed over both. Next, replace the textured fabrics with the original ones and gradually introduce prints. You will find that these create many illusions. Place a print that has white figures on a black ground on a white backing and see how the black recedes to a point where it appears to make holes in the fabric, often giving the appearance of lace. Finally, make a composition that consists entirely of black, white, and grays. Observe how much more texture you can satisfactorily incorporate here than in something that includes a variety of colors. The shades of gray should range gradually from almost white to almost black. Try to include at least five. You will find when you stand back that prints, tweeds and other mixtures of black and white or of black, white, and gray count as various shades of gray. Place these tones where they balance each other. See if you can arrange your darks so that they form a setting for the lights (or vice versa). Test this by putting a finger anywhere on a somber tone. You should be able to move it all around most of the dark area without lifting it from the background. Lastly, put a small spot of very bright color anywhere on the composition and see how it tends to become the center of interest.

Very large appliqués with complicated edges, such as those found in Hawaiian quilts or molas, are best handled in a very different manner. This method can be demonstrated in miniature by using 7-inch squares of cloth which have been straightened and made grain perfect. Fold and cut designs in 5-inch squares of paper, as shown in Figures 3-16 to 3-21. Do not make too many or too elaborate cuts, and make several trials until you have a design you really like.

Lay the cutout in position on the square of cloth that will be used for the appliqué. Pin it in place. You can simply trace around it with a pencil, including any cutouts in the center. However, using a row of stitching instead, whether hand or machine stitching, forms a hard line which strengthens the seamline and makes it not only easier to turn under the seam allowances, but permits far greater accuracy than otherwise. Do not stop or start the stitching at a difficult spot such as a point. If sewing by hand, use a small running stitch. This method also has the advantage of leaving no marks in most fabrics. A pencil line is usually easy to hide in ordinary appliqué, but it does not allow you to change your mind.

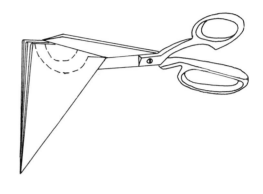

Fig. 3-20. Cutting out a shape.

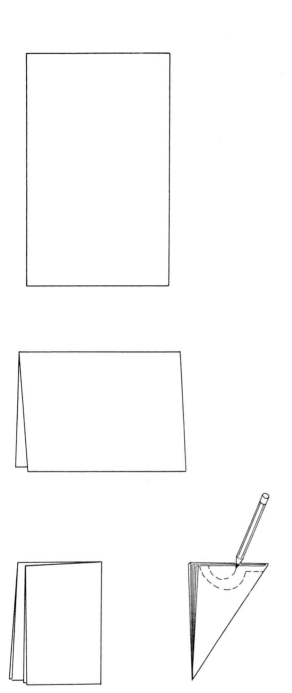

Fig. 3-21. The cutout.

Figs. 3-16, 3-17, 3-18, and 3-19. Folding paper. Mark in the
design with a pencil if desired.

Place the design square on the square of cloth that will form the background, with the lengthwise grain of both going in the same direction. Pin the two together and then baste carefully inside the design lines, keeping all basting 1/4-inch inside the seamline so it will not interfere with the hemming. Baste as shown in Figure 3-1, using enough stitches so that no part of the shape will shift. Baste across the shape and not around the edges, which might cause the patch to puff up. Leaving a seam allowance of 1/8-inch or slightly more, cut the outline of the shape and any internal cutouts. Clip the seam allowance up to the pencil line or stitching and hem. Clip as much as necessary, but do not make unnecessary cuts. Where the stitching is too tight to hide, clip through the thread only, but do not enlarge the cut in the fabric. Finish by hemming the appliqué with the help of a toothpick.

You can learn more about design using these same paper cutouts. The simpler the appliqué, the more important is the proportion of design to background. Cut the same shape in three or four sizes and place them one by one on a foundation square. Notice how equal proportions of design and background are not as satisfactory as when one or the other dominates. A very small design on a very large background gives a feeling of space or loneliness, especially if it is placed near a lower corner. Another consideration is the shape of the background. This is usually referred to as negative space and is as important as the foreground to your composition. Cut several different appliqués that are in good proportion to the background and concentrate on the negative space to see how attractive or interesting it is. Using black-and-white paper, make a counterchanging design in which the dark sections are indentical to the light sections. One way to do this is to cut identical sections from each and transpose them so that each lies on the other color.

Tracing and Transferring

When, instead of making paper cutouts, you draw the design for an elaborate appliqué of this type on paper, use artists' tracing paper. After the design is finished, pin the tracing paper to the appliqué fabric and stitch through design and fabric. You can then tear the paper away, thus leaving the stitched design in the fabric. Some people prefer to use tissue paper, since it tears away more easily and with less displacement of stitches. Tracing paper, however, allows erasure after erasure, which is a distinct advantage. Tighten up any loose stitches by pulling them up from the wrong side. The pattern can also be drawn directly on the fabric or transferred to it by means of carbon paper. But, again, the stitched line has many advantages over a pencil or carbon line.

When the design will only partially cover the background, transfer it to an oblong of appliqué fabric which is just large enough for the pattern plus seam allowance and which has been properly straightened. Line up the grain of the appliqué fabric and the grain of the background, pinning them very carefully together so that they will not shift. Then baste the appliqué.

Inlay

Inlay is usually best handled by stitching the design on the background fabric. Cut away the excess and match the grain as you lay small pieces of contrasting fabric underneath. In self-appliqué techniques with transparent fabrics, you can place the design under the fabric and draw it directly onto the sheer fabric with a pencil, or you can paint it on. Do not use stitching here unless you intend to cover the outline completely.

Where to Look for Ideas

Beginners who want to know where to look for ideas for their needlework usually do not realize that the ability to find designs grows with experience and that the important thing is to make a start by getting to work on a specific project. The horizon expands as you approach it, and each project that you carry out will not only help generate other ideas, but will also help you to understand what you see as you look at other people's work, thus sparking off further new thoughts. That does not mean that you copy what others do. When you see something you like, think how you can change it to come up with something unique.

Much appliqué is based on the manipulation of shapes, and these are everywhere. You can begin with simple geometrics and objects from nature that you can trace around, like leaves. Two lengthwise cuts in half an apple or pear (in the same plane that halved the fruit originally) gives three related shapes of different sizes. Or, you can make paper cutouts of all sorts. It is great fun to devise free-form shapes, which are characterized by curved outlines that change direction frequently and often radically. Books of devices and other geometrical drawings are rich sources of ideas for appliqué designs. Wrought-iron fences and other decorative ironwork has also been used successfully for inspiration. Drawing one's own designs is discouraged by many teachers who have been unable to get students to understand that, to be suitable for embroidery, drawings must be very simple, or drawing one's own designs is bypassed with the idea that it is too hard for beginners. Certainly many of us, educated along conservative pedagogical principles, became discouraged too early when we were asked to make faithful representations of objects on paper before our motor and mental skills were well developed. Most adults can, however, with a little practice, draw the *outlines* of many

of the things they see. And there is a vast difference between using your own drawing in a composition and using a tracing of someone else's. You will get better with practice, and remember, too, that rhythm plays an almost magical part in art, and a rhythmic repeat of a shape can enhance its beauty.

Having decided upon one or two basic shapes, cut out examples of them in various sizes in light cardboard. Using the smaller shapes as patterns, cut holes in some of the larger shapes. Explode some of the figures by making several cuts across them and spreading them apart, or rearrange and reassemble the cut sections. In cutting shapes apart, you get much more interesting results if, instead of using straight lines to make your cuts, you select interesting parts of the figure outline, and draw them across the shape to use as cutting guides. Use the cardboard shapes as templates, cutting more in different sizes as it seems necessary, and then apply the patches by creasing with an iron as described earlier (see fig. 3-9). If you are making a picture, it does not matter if your composition is non-objective or if it represents something tangible. It can also, like much contemporary art, represent a closeup of a small area of a tangible object. For practice stay away from symmetrical arrangements and, instead, try keeping the two halves of your foundation different but balanced. Offset a large area of dull blue on one side with a small area of bright color on the other. Take two pieces of the same color and intensity but of different sizes and see how close to the center of the picture each has to be to balance the other. Balance different textures in similar fashion.

Once you are satisfied with the placement of the basic shapes, you can, if you like, decorate the larger ones with rhythmic repeats of smaller cutouts. If you superimpose embroidery on your appliqué, try to exploit its textural values and not just its linear ones.

4.

Mola-Making: Pure Appliqué–and Hardly a Scrap of Fabric Wasted!

I have seen hundreds of molas, many of them complete blouses, from various places in San Blas, many dating from early in the century, and only a minute fraction of these could have been made by reverse appliqué, a process which has mistakenly been described as the traditional mola-making process. Certain traditional three-color molas are made by reverse appliqué (see Chapter 5), but any other occurrences either seemed to reflect the fact that the mola-maker did not have as many shades of cloth on hand as she might have liked or were attempts at a kind of simplification which has become more and more common since about 1969 or 1970.

The classic mola is pure appliqué and is distinguished by alternating bands of color. In a two-color panel, and these are always linear, with the lines sometimes suggesting figures, background and appliqué form lines of equal width that alternate with each other (see fig. 2-20). In a three-color mola (and these, too, are linear), the background generally alternates first with the second color and then with the third (see fig. 2-19). In most four-color linear molas, the structure is exactly the same as that in a three-color panel except that the lines of the appliqués are made wider and a fourth color is superimposed directly on top of them, leaving only about 1/8-inch of these lower appliqués showing on either side of it (see fig. 2-14). This same rule of alternation applies in a four-color panel even when the lines are bent around to enclose shapes (see fig. 4-27). That is why, in molas that depict large figures in their centers, the middle layer or layers that underlie the design are in colors different from the middle layer or layers that underlie the surrounding area (see color plate C-1) and, if there are more figures in the four corners, these, too, match the colors of the one in the center while the area between them is in a contrasting color.

Fig. 4-1. Cuna woman sewing a mola panel. (Courtesy of the photographer, the Reverend John Enright.)

Fig. 4-2. A three-color mola panel. The appliqués, which are of
two colors, are sewn to the background and not on top of each
other. Here two lines of a single color are not always separated
from each other by a line of the other hue as they generally
are now, which suggests that it is an early mola. (Courtesy of the
Field Museum of Natural History, Chicago, Illinois.)

I want to stress that the mola-making technique described on the following pages is not exactly the same as the one used by the Indian women, although, unlike reverse appliqué, it will produce a product identical with theirs if one chooses to copy. My problem was very much like that of the author of a cookbook whose great grandmother's "by guess and by golly" recipes have to be translated into exact measurements and instructions. Furthermore, I believe the method given here not only provides some insight into the way the more complicated forms of the mola may have evolved, but it is also probably the easiest for those who like to draw their designs on paper first. How the Cuna actually work is discussed at the end of this chapter, and it will be more easily understood after reading the following section.

In using the instructions below for the first time, work very accurately, measuring carefully and penciling in all the lines before cutting, because the seam allowances are very narrow and there is often no extra material. Should you accidentally cut a basting stitch, secure it immediately. The samples in the illustrations are miniatures, the largest being 7½-inches square. Do not experiment with large pieces; mola-making is extremely time consuming.

Fig. 4-3. Cushion made from a mola panel that is an alternate form of the three-color mola. Here one of the appliqués is sewn on top of the other. This is the only kind of mola with more than two colors that does not have a mosaic layer. The one shown is a contemporary design, but this type of mola was found much more frequently in the early days. (Courtesy of Clive and Olivia Dorman.)

The Two-Color Mola

We know that the mola began as a simple band of appliqué, and this form survives in the two-color mola. Cut a piece of artists' tracing paper and two pieces of cloth in colors that contrast with each other so that you have one of each of the three, all the same size and shape. This may be a rectangle as in a mola or part of a pattern for a garment. Leaving ⅝-inch or more all around for a border, draw a pencil design on tracing paper. Cover the available space as well as you can, keeping all lines at least ½-inch apart. There is no need to make ¼-inch thick lines on the drawing; an ordinary thin pencil line will do (fig. 4-5), and the basting line it marks will widen because each edge turns back for stitching. By the time the piece is completed, the thin pencil lines will become thick lines of appliqué. The pictures of two-color molas in this book will give you some ideas about the pattern. Getting a coherent design of this sort is not as easy as it looks, especially if you make each of the four quarters all a bit different from each other but still try to keep them in balance, so expect to keep changing parts of the drawing until it is satisfactory. Then, before going on, make a second copy since the original will be destroyed as you work with it.

Sandwich the piece of cloth that is to become the appliqué (Layer 2) between the tracing-paper pattern and the piece that will form the background (Layer 1), with the paper on top. The drawing should be face up. Pin or baste these three layers together around the edges and anywhere else that seems necessary in order to keep them

Fig. 4-4. Samplers. Quarter-size panels based on, but not direct copies of, four genuine molas. *Upper left:* a two-color mola; *upper right:* the more common form of three-color mola; *lower left:* a four-color linear mola; *lower right:* a four-color mola based on an objective design with inlay fillings.

from slipping or puffing up. These basting stitches can be quite large and how many you put in will depend upon the size of your piece. Now, working very accurately, transfer the design to the fabric by basting through all three layers, paper included. Baste along every bit of the design line, this time using small stitches and thread that matches the appliqué, since a contrasting color may leave lint behind in the holes when the stitches are removed. Note that the outer edge of the design (or the inner line of the border) is also part of the design and must also be basted, so that the border area will be the same color as the appliqué, not the color of the background. Begin with a knot too large to pull through the fabric and end with two back stitches taken one over the other. Get into the habit of keeping these at the back of the work. It does not matter in a two-color mola, but in more complicated ones, the lumpy knots can be trapped inside the layers where they cannot be cut off. Be sure to indicate accurately where lines begin or end and where they form angles. You may prefer to do this basting on the sewing machine. If so, pull all the ends through to the back of the work and tie them together or it will be difficult to decide later where lines start and finish.

When the entire design has been covered with the small basting stitches, remove the pins or the large basting stitches put in earlier. Carefully tear away the tracing paper, trying to displace the small basting stitches as little as possible. Stretch the piece flat with both hands and pull any loose stitches to the back. Your cutting line is midway between the basting lines as it will always be in these linear examples. Your seam allowance will be only ⅛-inch wide, so pencil in the cutting line accurately before starting to snip, using small, sharp-pointed embroidery scissors. Cut through the top layer only, being very careful not to pierce the background. When you come to an angle, clip only halfway into the corner as shown in Figure 4-5. After turning under and hemming your ⅛-inch seam allowance, you will have a design line ¼-inch wide. Notice that no fabric has been cut away except for small snippets to aid in turning under when the lines of the design are curved.

In subsequent trials, the lines can be thickened in places to make a design like that in Figure 4-3, and, if desired, the resulting shapes can be embellished with a third color by using the slit-and-inlay technique (see figs. 4-22 and 4-23), embroidery, etc.

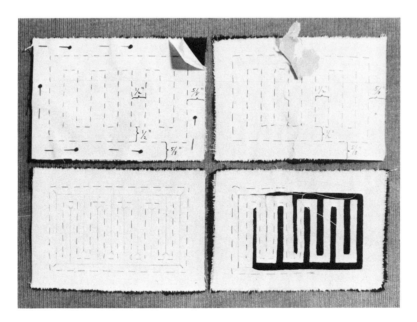

Fig. 4-5. Making the two-color mola. *Upper left:* the design, which has been drawn on tracing or tissue paper, is put on top of two layers of cloth that contrast in color. Basting stitches, which carefully follow the lines of the design are taken through all three layers. *Upper right:* the paper is torn away leaving the stitches in the cloth. *Lower left:* pencil lines to guide the cuttings are made halfway between the bastings. *Lower right:* only the top layer is cut and the corners are clipped into halfway only. The hems are turned under and stitched.

The Three-Color Mola

Proceed as for the two-color mola, this time collecting three pieces of cloth in different colors. Now the lines drawn on the tracing paper must be a full 1-inch apart (fig. 4-6). Stack only two layers of cloth and the paper with the drawing. (Don't forget to make a copy of the drawing.) The third piece of material (Layer 3) is held aside for the moment. It will be put on the stack later. The cloth that is to form the background of the mola (Layer 1) is once more placed on the bottom of the pile.

Again baste or pin all three layers together with large stitches around the edges and wherever else it is needed. Then, with small, careful stitches, baste along the design line, again including the inner part of the border. Remove the large basting stitches or pins and tear the paper away. Your cutting line this time also lies midway between the basting lines. Pencil it in and again cut along it, piercing only the top layer. Trim all seams to ¼-inch wide. In subsequent trials, you may hem immediately, but *do not remove the bastings* nevertheless, for they will be used as guides in the next step. For now, continue without hemming, since that will help you to learn more about the cutting lines in the mola.

Now take the third piece of cloth that you cut out and put aside at the beginning (Layer 3). Cover the face of your work with it (fig. 4-7). Baste all three layers together around the edges (pins will get in the way this time), and turn the work over so that it is face down. Working on the wrong side, with a pencil, draw lines midway between the bastings. With small, careful basting stitches, sew all three layers together along these penciled lines. Turn the work over again so that it is face up.

The new cutting line is again halfway between the basting lines and ½-inch beyond the outermost basting lines that are visible on the face of the work. Pencil it in and cut along it as before, again being careful to cut the top layer only (fig. 4-8). Trim the seams in the top layer to

Fig. 4-6. Making the three-color mola (part 1). *Upper left:* stack two cloth layers with the tracing paper design on top as for a two-layer mola, but hold aside a third layer as shown at upper right. Baste through the design, going through tissue paper and two layers. Tear away the paper. *Lower left:* cut only the top layer midway between the bastings. *Lower right:* trim seams to ¼-inch wide.

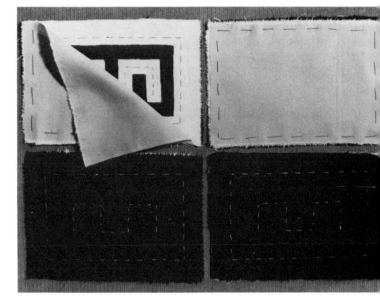

Fig. 4-7. Making the three-color mola (part 2). *Upper left and right:* take the layer that was held aside (Fig. 4-6, upper right), place it directly over the face of your work, and baste the layers together around the edges. *Lower left:* turn work to wrong side. *Lower right:* make a second line of basting stitches midway between those already there.

¼-inch wide. Remove only the large bastings around the edge and discard the outer rim of the top layer that falls away as they are removed.

Stop now and look at your work. There are three or more separate appliqués, depending on the size of your panel, ready to be sewn down to a common background. They entirely cover that background without overlapping or gaping, and the two colors in the top layer alternate in the way that is characteristic of molas. You might say that, before hemming, the three-color mola consists of two layers, the lower one a solid piece of cloth and the upper one a mosaic of two colors that covers exactly the same area as the first. Figure 4-9, lower left, shows the pieces that were cut away when the seams were trimmed. Had you snipped them as the Indians do, along the cutting lines only, you would have three or more appliqués, exactly like the first set but reversed in color (fig. 4-9, lower right). These could also be sewn to a background the same color as the first, and that is what many Cuna

women do. One panel becomes the front of the blouse and the other the back, or you might use them in two different blouses. It should be obvious that the two top layers have the same cutting line and that you could also make this mola by stacking them, snipping both of them apart along it, separating the resulting pieces, and reassembling them on two backgrounds of identical color.

Clip halfway into the corners and hem the appliqués as before, turning under ⅛-inch and sewing them down to the background. Remove the bastings.

All molas of four or more colors are based upon this three-color panel. When more colors are to be added, they are superimposed on its appliqués, which are made wider so that upper and lower colors both show. There is also a less-common variant of the three-color mola which does not have a mosaic layer (see fig. 4-3.)

Fig. 4-8. Making the three-color mola (part 3). *Upper left:* turn work to right side. *Upper right:* cut only the top layer midway between the bastings. Trim seams in top layer to ¼-inch wide. *Below:* Hem the appliqués.

Fig. 4-9. *Above:* this is the same as Figure 4-8, upper right. *Lower left:* the six pieces that were trimmed away using the method above. *Lower right:* the three extra pieces that are left when cutting Layers 2 and 3 the Indian way along a common cutting line. They are exactly the same as the top mosaic but reversed in color and can be used as the upper layer in another three-color panel.

The Four-Color Linear Mola

If you have been working with small samples like mine, you will have to make this one larger, for this time the basting lines in the drawing need to be 1½-inches apart (fig. 4-10). Don't forget to make a copy of the drawing. The procedure is similar to that used for the three-color mola.

Cut four pieces of cloth in four different colors all the same size and shape as the tracing-paper drawing. Stack and baste together two cloth layers (Layers 1 & 2) with the drawing on top and set aside the other two (Layers 3 & 4). Baste along the design line through all three layers as before. Tear away the tissue. Cut through only the top layer halfway between the basting stitches. This time trim the seams to ⅜-inch wide.

Place one of the two remaining pieces of cloth (Layer 3) over the face of your work, still keeping aside the piece you want for the uppermost layer (Layer 4). Baste all three layers together all around the edges and turn the work face down.

Draw in the second basting lines midway between the first set. Baste carefully through all layers and turn the work face up.

Cut only the top layer halfway between the basting lines. Trim the seams to ⅜-inch wide. Remove the large bastings from around the edge and discard the fabric that falls away.

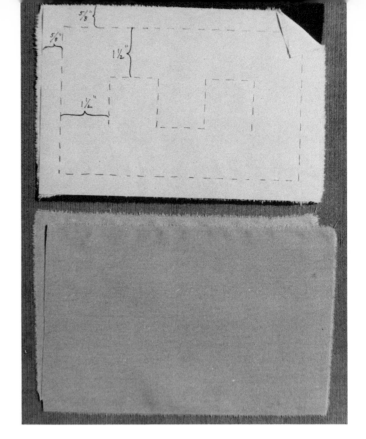

Fig. 4-10. Making a four-color linear mola (part 1). Cut four cloth layers and hold two aside (lower part of picture). Work as before until a three-color mola has been completed but not hemmed. Trim seams of Layers 2 and 3 to ⅜-inch wide.

Fig. 4-11. Making a four-color linear mola (part 2). *Upper left:* place the fourth layer over the face of the work and baste the layers together. *Upper right:* turn work to wrong side and baste again over all the bastings visible on the reverse side going through all the layers. *Lower left:* turn the panel face up. Cut only the top layer midway between the bastings. Trim all seams in this layer to ¼-inch wide. *Lower right:* hem.

74

Again cover the face of the work with the piece of fabric reserved for the uppermost layer (Layer 4). Baste the layers together around the edges, and turn the work face down. This time, baste carefully a second time over all of the sets of bastings visible on this reverse side, going through all of the layers (fig. 4-11). Be sure the ends of all lines and the corners will be marked accurately on the right side of the work. Turn the panel face up. Cut only the top layer midway between the bastings. Trim all the seams in this layer only to ¼-inch wide. Turn under all hems ⅛-inch and sew them down. Remove the bastings.

This is the most common structure for a four-color linear mola, but there are some to be found, especially early ones, where the fourth layer is superimposed only on one color of the first appliqué layer and not the other (fig. 4-12). In that case, the uncovered stripe is made a ¼-inch wide instead of ½-inch wide, as in the common form. The lines of the drawing for such a panel must be placed 1¼-inch apart. Work exactly as for the previous four-color mola, but, after cutting Layer 3, trim the seams to a ¼-inch wide instead of ⅜-inch wide. After basting Layer 4 to the face of the work and turning the piece to the wrong side, baste only along the set of bastings that will carry the superimposed appliqué. Turn face up, cut midway between the bastings, trim the seams of the uppermost layer ¼-inch wide, and hem.

The same remarks apply to these two molas that applied to the three-color mola. The same cutting lines are common to all layers except the bottom one, which remains intact. The four-color panel might be looked upon as a three-layer appliqué in which the middle layer is a mosaic of two colors. If you work only with the cutting line as the Indians do, you could stack the three top layers, cut them out all at once, and you would wind up with a duplicate set of the middle layer with the colors reversed. The Cuna women not only incorporate these in panels with top and bottom layers identical to the first mola, but they also like to reverse these outer layers sometimes, putting the one that was above below, and vice versa.

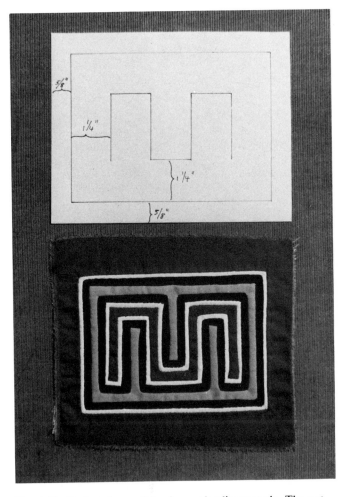

Fig. 4-12. Variant form of the four-color linear mola. The pattern is shown at the top and the completed panel at the bottom. Work exactly like the previous four-color mola but, after cutting Layer 3, trim the seams to ¼-inch instead of ⅜-inch. After basting Layer 4 to the face of the work and turning the piece to the wrong side, baste only along the set of bastings that will carry the superimposed appliqué. Turn face up and cut midway between the bastings as usual.

The Four-Color Mola That Depicts an Object

Begin with a simple outline shape suitable for appliqué. Draw this on tracing paper (fig. 4-13, upper left), making a duplicate copy in case you should want to repeat the design. Stack your layers as before with the one you ultimately want on the bottom first (Layer 1), the one you want to underlie your figure next (Layer 2), and the tracing, face up, on top. Baste these together around the edges with large stitches and then, with small careful ones, baste all along the pencil line. Tear away the tracing paper. Cut out only the top layer ¼-inch outside the basting, going all around the figure. Set aside the excess fabric that falls away.

Baste Layer 3 in place over the face of the work and turn the piece over (fig. 4-14). Draw a pencil line on the wrong side going all around the figure, ½-inch outside the stitch-ing. Baste carefully along this line and turn the work face up again. After the panel is turned face up, cut through the top layer only. The cutting line is ¼-inch inside the basting. Cut along it and set aside the central piece that falls free. Again the two discarded pieces are the reverse of the center mosaic and again they could be used for a second mola identical with the first except for the reversed colors.

Place the fourth layer over the face of the work and baste the layers together all around the edges (fig. 4-15). Turn the work over. Baste all around the inside of the shape, ⅛-inch inside the original basting, and baste all around the outer basting line, again ⅛-inch away from it. Turn the work face up. Again, after the panel is turned, cut through the top layer only. Cut halfway between the two rows of bastings and trim both seams in the uppermost layer to ¼-inch wide. Turn under all raw edges ⅛-inch and hem them. Notice that, when hemmed, the central

Fig. 4-13. Making the four-color mola that depicts an object (part 1). *Upper right:* hold two layers aside. *Upper left:* baste the other two layers and the tissue paper design together both around the edges and along the design line going through all three layers. *Lower left:* tear away the paper. *Lower right:* cut out only the top layer, ¼-inch outside the basting going all around the figure.

Fig. 4-14. Making the four-color mola that depicts an object (part 2). *Upper right:* continue to hold the fourth layer aside. *Upper left:* baste Layer 3 over the face of the work. *Lower left:* turn the piece over. Baste ½-inch outside the stitching, going all around the figure. *Lower right:* turn work right side up. The cutting line is ¼-inch inside the basting.

figure in the top layer is the same size as your original tracing. When making a panel with more than one figure, they should be ½-inch apart where they come closest to each other in the tracing-paper drawing. Details such as eyes, may be added by means of inlay, appliqué, or embroidery.

Here again, the top three layers could be snipped out all at once along the common cutting line which is located ¼-inch outside the traced line of the drawing, and the unwanted duplicate parts of the inner layers removed (fig. 4-16). While I do not find it particularly easy to handle linear patterns this way because I am forced to think in terms of the cutting line rather than the design line, it is a simpler method when dealing with designs that depict objects.

Look again at the four-layer sample. The figure is formed by the top layer. This is ringed with ⅛-inch bor-

der in a contrasting color, outside of which there is a ¼-inch ring of the background color. The next ring introduces the fourth color before the one in the top layer is repeated. This is characteristic of the basic structure of the classic mola. There are always two *different* colors on either side of the bottommost layer whenever it is visible on the face of the panel. Thus, if there were two fish facing each other with a smaller object between them, the color underlying the central object would match the one that underlies the negative space surrounding the fish and would contrast with the color that underlies them. This corresponds to the alternating lines of color in the linear molas. Figures 4-17 to 4-21 show how the colors of the inner layer are usually distributed in molas that depict objects.

Fig. 4-15. Making the four-color mola that depicts an object (part 3). *Upper left:* baste the fourth layer over the face of the work. *Upper right:* turn the piece over. Baste all around the inside of the shape, ⅛-inch inside the original basting and all around the outer basting line, again ⅛-inch away from it. *Lower left:* turn work face up. Cut the top layer only halfway between the two rows of basting and trim both seams in the upper layer to ¼-inch wide. Turn under all raw edges ⅛-inch and hem. *Lower right:* the completed figure. Inlay and other fillings would normally be worked inside the fish and on the background to complete the panel.

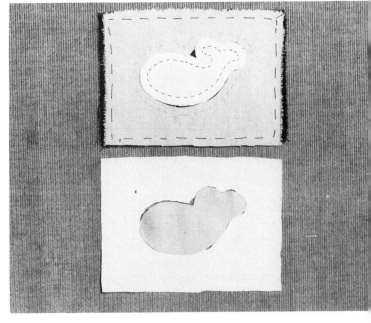

Fig. 4-16. The discarded parts of the mola described above are shown at the bottom of the photograph. This time they are not fragmented whether or not the Indian method is followed. Again they form the reverse of the mosaic layer shown at the top of the photograph and could be included in a second panel.

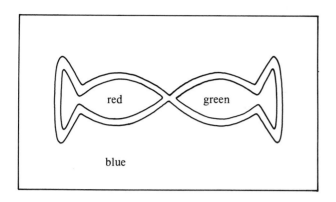

In molas based on lines, because of the nature of the design, the space in the panel is always well filled. In molas with figures, this does not happen automatically and various devices are resorted to to clothe the empty background. Embroidery is one of these, small appliqués sewn to the top layer another, but more often, many small pieces of fabric in a rainbow of extra colors are placed under slits or shapes which are cut into the top layer. This device is typical only of molas of four or more colors that depict objects.

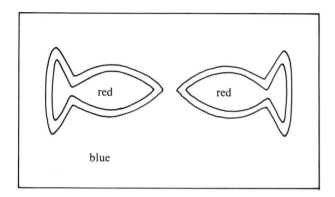

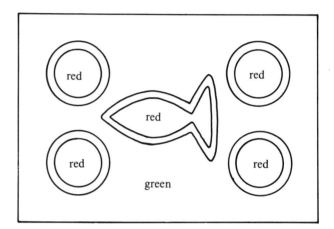

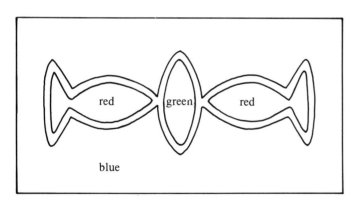

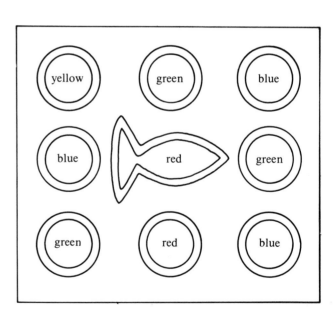

Figs. 4-17, 4-18, 4-19, 4-20, and 4-21. How the inner mosaic layer is distributed in various situations.

One of the most common kinds of inlay of this sort is one I have dubbed the "slit-and-inlay" technique. It consists of making straight cuts in the top layer of the mola. So that the edges of these can be turned back and hemmed down, "v"s are cut at top and bottom of each slit (see fig. 4-22). A similar device that is also seen frequently is a cluster of "v"s. These must also be snipped further so that the edges can be turned back (see fig. 4-23). A group of small circles is another favorite, but squares, triangles and many other shapes are made. Usually the little rectangles of cloth that are pushed under these shapes before they are closed by hemming are made to underlie two, three or more of the openings rather than just one. The Indian women frequently position these extra pieces before doing any sewing at all. When putting on the layers one at a time, if such openings are to be small, such as a group of tiny circles, it may be necessary to look ahead and position the inlay rectangles before the area is closed off. This is especially true if it occurs in the middle of the panel, but if it is at the edge, it may only be necessary to remove a few of the bastings if the mola-maker had forgotten to plan ahead for its placement.

Often, as in the center and all four corners of the sampler in the lower right-hand corner of Figure 4-4, other colors are substituted for the middle layer. This is extremely time-consuming, but simple to do since you merely snip away the unwanted part of the middle layer and slip an extra rectangle of cloth under the top layer before hemming it down. The insert is then hemmed first. The method is obvious if the photograph is examined carefully.

All these extra colors in the inlays make it difficult to know how many actual basic layers there are in a given mola. To find out, count the top layer as "one." Then find a place where the lowest layer is exposed on the face of the panel, preferably where it outlines a major shape, and count that as "two." Next add in the number of different colors in the inner layers that show on both sides of the exposed bottom layer before you get back to the top layer. Inlaid pieces are always placed directly under the top layer, and that helps to identify them.

Saw-toothed lines are frequently found in molas. The teeth may lie on one or both sides of the appliqué line. They, too, are very time-consuming and they also take a certain amount of practice in order to do them well (see figs. 3-11 and 3-12). Make them as in Figure 4-24. Sometimes the Cuna women substitute rickrack for this, but it is generally not as visually striking as saw-toothed appliqué.

Fig. 4-22. Cuts for the slit-and-inlay technique must have "v"s at top and bottom so the edges can be turned back. A rectangle of cloth is placed underneath before hemming so that its contrasting color shows through. Usually a rectangle underlies at least two or three slits.

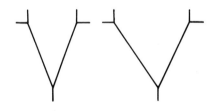

Fig. 4-23. How to snip the "v"s for inlay.

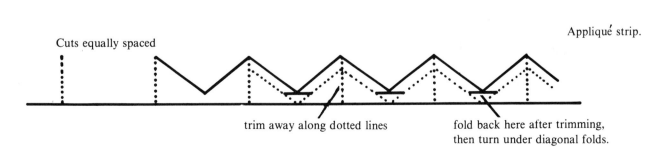

Appliqué strip.

Cuts equally spaced

trim away along dotted lines

fold back here after trimming, then turn under diagonal folds.

Fig. 4-24. How to snip for a sawtoothed line.

The Six-Color Mola

Figure 4-25 shows a six-color linear mola. The fourth layer is superimposed over the second and the fifth over the third. Layer 6 lies over both the fourth and fifth layers. The lines of the drawing for this kind of mola need to be spaced 2-inches apart, and the second and fourth layers can be put on at one time with a single set of bastings (fig. 4-25, lower left) as can the third and fifth. This panel can be thought of as a four-layer appliqué in which the two middle layers are both two-color mosaics. Cutting it the Indian way by stacking all but the bottom layer and using the set of cutting lines that is common to all the others, duplicates of the two middle layers with reversed colors can be obtained to use elsewhere.

To design a six-color mola that depicts an object keep all the shapes ¾-inch apart where they are nearest to each other. The cutting line is ⅜-inch from the outlines of the figures. To make it by adding the layers one or two at a time, stack Layers 1, 2, and 4 with the tracing on top. After basting and tearing the paper away, trim the fourth layer to ¼-inch and the second layer to ⅜-inch. Next, put on Layers 3 and 5 at one time, using only one set of bastings for both. Trim Layer 5 to ¼-inch and Layer 3 to ⅜-inch. Add the uppermost layer, turn the work over, and baste all around the inside of the shapes ⅛-inch inside the original bastings, and baste all around the outer basting lines (the ones that hold Layers 3 and 5), again ⅛-inch away from it. Turn the work face up, cut halfway between the two rows of bastings, and trim all seams in the uppermost layer to ¼-inch wide. Hem.

The Indian Method

After having practiced making two-, three-, four-, and six-color molas, the reader should have some insight into the general method used in mola-making by the Cuna. Figures 4-26 to 4-29 are even more revealing. They show various aspects of a panel in progress, and its mate which is nearer to completion. While there are variations in the way different women work, we have already discussed their fundamental technique of working in terms of the basic cutting line. This is relatively simple and it is the same for all the layers in any given mola or pair of molas.

The Indians generally cut the design directly into the cloth, though some may mark it out first with a pencil. A few have been reported to use splinters of bamboo as gauges to determine how far apart the lines should be. The Indians got scissors and needles from coconut boats in trade since the mid-nineteenth century when mola-making began. To keep cutout shapes from falling away during the preliminaries, one of two devices is resorted to. Either the design is cut out only partially and the sewing in the section involved completed or almost completed before going on to do more cutting elsewhere, or an interrupted snipping technique is employed (fig. 4-30). The unsnipped "bridges" are cut later as they are reached in the sewing.

Fig. 4-25. Making the six-color linear mola. The second and fourth layers can be put on with the same line of basting stitches as can the third and fifth.

Fib. 4-26. A four-color objective mola panel. This panel may be complete, but most Indians have additional fillings of some sort in a large central figure. (Courtesy of the Field Museum of Natural History, Chicago, Illinois.)

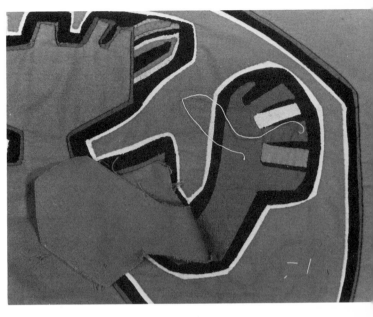

Fig. 4-27. A panel which is the mate to the one shown in Figure 4-26. This one is only partially completed. The unhemmed portion of the top layer is turned back to show that the section underneath has already been finished and that the mola is being sewn from the bottom up. Examine the circles around the central figure in this and the previous photograph. The colors are reversed, showing that the parts of the middle mosaic layer not needed for the first were incorporated into the second. (Courtesy of the Field Museum of Natural History, Chicago, Illinois.)

Fig. 4-28. Closeup of the panel shown in Figure 4-27. (Courtesy of the Field Museum of Natural History, Chicago, Illinois.)

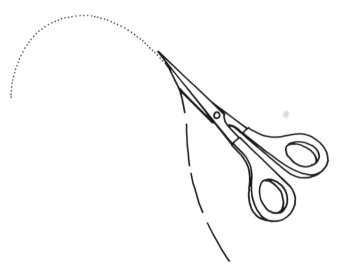

Fig. 4-29. Reverse side of the incomplete panel in Figure 4-27. The bastings indicate that the rectangles for the slit-and-inlay fillings (see Figure 4-26) were basted to the lower layers before the top layer was put on. (Courtesy of the Field Museum of Natural History, Chicago, Illinois.)

Fig. 4-30. The interrupted snipping used by the Indians.

Pins are not used, and the layers are put together with many basting stitches which are snipped away as they get in the way of the sewing. Unfortunately, every one of the firsthand accounts tries to summarize all the mola-making processes regardless of how many layers are involved, and it is impossible to tell for sure exactly how the inner mosaic layer or layers are handled. Even a number of people who have lived and worked among the Cuna and who, because of their interests, could be expected to have an answer, can give no details.

In a very brief correspondence with an Indian couple, I was told by them that two, three, and sometimes even four layers of fabric of the same size but different colors are laid one on top of the other. The designs are marked out, freehand, with scissors, on one or another of the pieces of cloth so that the layers show up where they are wanted. At the same time, fragment after fragment of cloth is inserted. This corresponds to what we see in Figure 4-27. The salient point is that, while the top layer of the mola is cut initially, the sewing itself is done from the bottom up. This, I cannot resist pointing out, is the very reverse of reverse appliqué.

Fig. 4-31 and 4-32. Two sides of the same blouse. The lines around the crosses and the figure of Christ show that the pieces of the double inner mosaic layer have been distributed between the two panels. (Courtesy of the Field Museum of Natural History, Chicago, Illinois.)

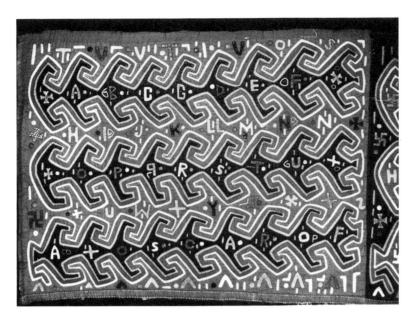

Fig. 4-33 and 4-34. "Alphabet" mola. Here the top layers have
been transposed. The panels are joined together at one side
and each photograph shows a small portion of the other panel.
(Courtesy of the Field Museum of Natural History, Chicago,
Illinois.)

Simplified Forms of the Mola

As we have seen, the demand for molas has far outrun the supply. Many simplified ones have been appearing, some of which are workmanlike and logical developments of this particular art form, but others are just hurry-up jobs with little to recommend them. Usually, there are fewer layers than before, and the alternation of colors is often sacrificed. Figure 4-35 and the small rectangle in color plate C-17 both show molas with designs that, in earlier times, were commonly made with four layers. Both have only two layers. The little tapir has colors beyond the two basic ones done in careful appliqué. Only about 5″ × 8″, it would make a charming pocket. The second mola has all the extra colors brought in as inlay. It is typical of many molas being marketed today.

Fig. 4-35. Simplified mola panel, early 1970s. This mola has only two layers and much inlay. (Courtesy of Neely Bostick.)

Fig. 4-36. A most unusual mola panel. (Courtesy of the Reverend
Leo T. Mahon.)

Fig. 4-37. This black-and-white beast with a red eye has no fillings worked in either figure or background. (Courtesy of Wilma Birkeland.)

Contemporary Work

We have talked much about the center mosaic layer or layers in the mola. This suggests an avenue for experimentation. Cut a piece of paper the size of your proposed panel. Divide this up with lines drawn fairly wide apart. Two simple suggestions are shown in Figures 4-38 and 4-39. Pin this to a stack of three pieces of cloth the same size as the pattern and of different colors. Cut through all layers along the lines drawn on the paper, but do not lose the order of the pieces. Reassemble the design, one layer deep, on a fourth piece of cloth, also the same size, mixing colors at will. Baste this composite layer to the full layer below it, and turn the raw edges under ⅛-inch. Hem. Repeat, placing a second layer over the first. Make the hems on this one ¼-inch wide. The third layer will have hems ⅜-inch wide. Using felt or colored paper until a satisfactory design is achieved would eliminate all the hemming. Many variations of this idea will come to mind. After piecing the pattern, more appliqué, inlay, embroidery, etc. can be used to decorate the completed layers.

The banners shown in color plates C-21, C-22, and C-23 are three of a larger group designed by artist Lillian Brulc when she lived in Panama. They are a direct study of the mola. The designer selected the cloth, laid the colors together (two shades of purple, for instance, with another color laid between them), folded it over and cut it. The sewing was done by the women of the church for which the banners were made. The earlier banners, including *Lent* and *Pentecost*, were done on the sewing machine. *Christmas* was one of the later ones which were hand sewn.

The artist says of her work, "I tried to capture the feeling of the molas—both in the method and in the response one gets when looking at them. Using several layers of cloth with a dominant motif and a dominant color scheme, I cut spontaneously following the rhythmical sequence and balance which I feel in the mola—a rhythmic sense of color to color and shape to shape. This procedure allowed for some of the surprise element that I find in almost every one of the Cuna designs, an unexpected bit of color or an unexpected turn in the pattern."

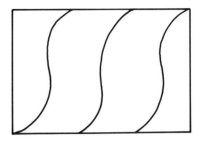

Figs. 4-38 and 4-39. Two simple suggestions for contemporary experiments.

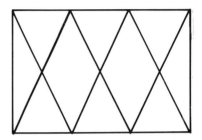

5.

Reverse Appliqué, a Fascinating By-Product

Essentially, *reverse appliqué* is the process that Americans mistakenly think the Cuna women use to make their blouse panels. For more than a dozen years in the United States, and now in England, many people who have not had the occasion or the opportunity to examine molas closely have been led to believe that reverse appliqué is the technique, and the only technique, by which they are produced.

Before 1963, pictures of molas appeared now and then in American books and periodicals, but there were almost no attempts to describe how they were made except occasionally to categorize them as appliqué. One gets the definite impression that nobody really wanted to venture a guess as to the complicated technique used. Then, a national magazine, *McCall's Needlework and Crafts*, courageously stuck its neck out. It reproduced three molas of the type whose physical configuration indicates to me that they were constructed as shown in the last chapter. It was explained that they were made by the method described later on in this chapter, and they were accompanied by a contemporary panel. It was suggested that reverse appliqué might be a suitable name for the process.

While the term "reverse appliqué" originated entirely with the magazine, the idea it represents may not have. From time to time, short statements have appeared in which first-hand observers have attempted to describe mola-making. Some of these may have been available in print in 1963, the time the magazine story was published. All of them are so brief (a sentence, or, at most a paragraph) and so vague that it is impossible to tell what the Indian women were actually doing although some of the statements do suggest an idea that could be construed as reverse appliqué.

The fact is that anyone who sits down and actually tests the theory by trying to copy a genuine multi-layer mola using reverse appliqué will find it could, perhaps, be accomplished in some cases, but only with great difficulty and lack of economy both of labor and cloth. As an explanation of what the Indians really do, it is, at best, a gross oversimplification.

However, reverse appliqué caught on and quickly became popular, not just because many people thought you could make a mola that way, but because it is great fun. If the magazine article did not explain the mola, we are nevertheless indebted to the editors for presenting us with a brand new craft idea.

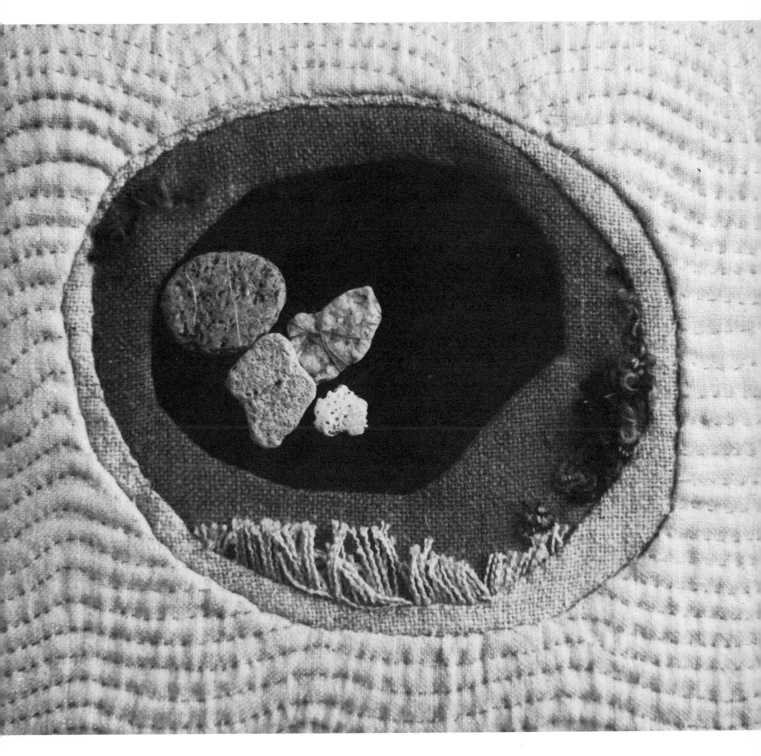

Fig. 5-1. *Tidal Pool*, by Martha P. Davenport. A very simple but expressive use of reverse appliqué. (Courtesy of the artist.)

How to Do Reverse Appliqué

Begin with the fabrics indicated in Chapter 3 as being easiest to use for appliqué. Solid-colored broadcloth is a good choice. Limit early experiments to bright, intense primary hues and their complements like those often used for painting children's furniture: red, yellow, blue, green, orange and purple. These provide the most fun at the outset and probably yield the most information, especially if two or three experiments are tried using the same set of colors stacked differently in each successive trial. As we will see later, large reverse appliqué panels present special problems, so keep the first pieces small—not much more than 8 × 10 inches.

Stack five pieces of cloth of identical size but different colors one on top of the other as shown in Figure 5-2. Baste the stack through all five thicknesses all around the edges being sure to keep everything perfectly flat (fig. 5-3). Cut one or more free-form or geometric shapes in the top layer (fig. 5-4), separating them a bit if there are more than one. Turn under and hem the raw edges that are left after the shape is taken away (fig. 5-5). Next, cut one or more shapes in the exposed second layer (fig. 5-6) and again finish the edges by hemming (fig. 5-7). Repeat until the bottom layer is reached (fig. 5-8). That is all there is to the basic technique.

Fig. 5-3. How to do reverse appliqué. Basting stack all around edges.

Fig. 5-2. How to do reverse appliqué. Stacking cloth.

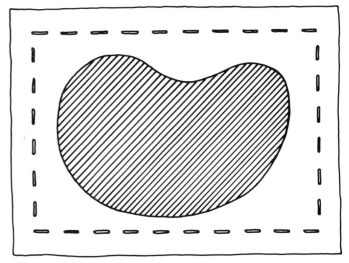

Fig. 5-4. How to do reverse appliqué. Cutting free-form shape in top layer.

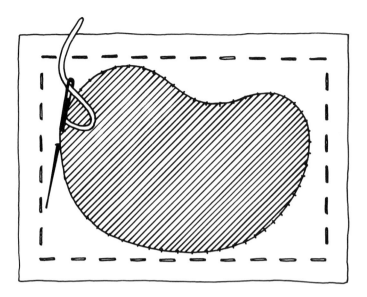

Fig. 5-5. How to do reverse appliqué. Hemming the edges of the shape.

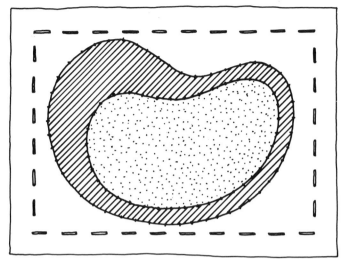

Fig. 5-7. How to do reverse appliqué. Hemming edges of shape in second layer.

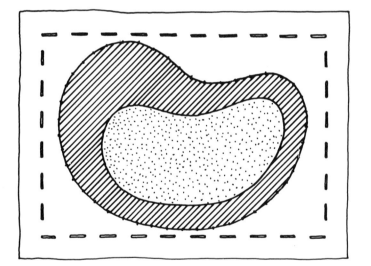

Fig. 5-6. How to do reverse appliqué. Cutting shape in exposed second layer.

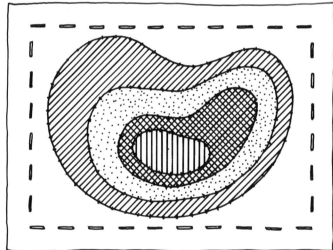

Fig. 5-8. How to do reverse appliqué. Continuing the cutting and hemming until lowest layer is exposed.

It becomes obvious immediately that the hems must be allowed for by making the shapes slightly smaller than the finished cutout is to be. And it soon becomes apparent also that shapes cannot be placed right next to each other without leaving room between them to turn under the hems, however narrow. Therefore, in designing for reverse appliqué, the drawing in Figure 5-9 must be modified to that shown in Figure 5-10, and the drawing in Figure 5-11 must be changed to look like Figure 5-12.

Layers may be bypassed or skipped. Simply cut them back far enough so that they do not show when the layer above them is hemmed down.

A cutout can be made to underlie portions of two or more other cutouts as shown at lower left in Figure 5-16. It takes a little preplanning, however, for you must reach in under the layer above with your scissors after that layer is cut but before it is hemmed down.

Small bits of cloth beyond the ones in the multiple layers originally stacked for any given piece can be introduced by using appliqué or the slit-and-inlay technique of the Cuna (see fig. 4-22).

One possibility that seems not to have occurred to many people is inspired by the sleeve of Tudor times that had slits cut into it through which a lining or the loose chemise worn underneath was pulled up to make decorative contrasting puffs. This can be done also in reverse appliqué as shown in the sample in Figure 5-13. Cut slits or small circles in the upper layer and finish them by hemming. Lay generous-sized pieces of cloth in a contrasting color under the slits and pull them up through the openings. Be sure to choose a fairly lightweight fabric that drapes nicely for the underlayer. When the desired effect is achieved, stitch around the openings through both layers and trim away the excess in the lower one (fig. 5-14). The puffs may be stuffed with dacron or cotton batting if desired. Keep the filling in place by closing the opening on the wrong side with herringbone stitch.

Wide ribbon or yarn could also be stitched to the lower layers and brought up to the surface through the holes. Two ends emerging from different openings could be tied together on the surface. Once the idea of pulling fabric and yarn up from below is conceived of, many new thoughts come to mind.

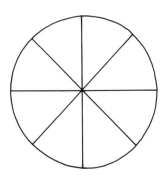

Fig. 5-9. Improper drawing for reverse appliqué.

Fig. 5-11. Another improper drawing for reverse appliqué.

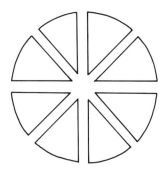

Fig. 5-10. The drawing corrected.

Fig. 5-12. The second drawing corrected.

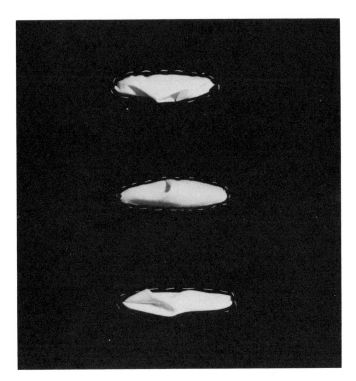

Fig. 5-13. The common sleeve of Tudor times, which had slits cut into it through which the loose chemise underneath was pulled up to make decorative puffs, inspired this reverse appliqué sample. Here white fabric has been pulled up through slits in a black background. The white stitching shows where the two layers are joined together.

Fig. 5-14. Reverse side of the sample in Figure 5-13. After sewing, the excess parts of the lower layer have been cut away to reduce bulk. The puffs could be stuffed from this side and closed with herringbone stitch if desired.

Fig. 5-13a. Portrait of Morette, a French envoy to the court of Henry VIII, painted by Hans Holbein, the younger. The parts of the sleeves that cover the forearm are slashed so that the white garment beneath may be pulled up to form decorative puffs in a style typical of the period. (Courtesy Gemäldgalerie, Dresden. Reproduced from the collection of the Library of Congress.)

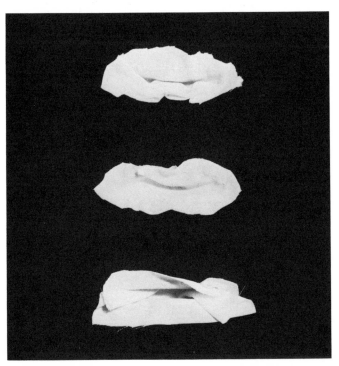

When making wall hangings, table tops, and so forth, one or more of the layers can be separated from the others by ¾-inch widths or more. This adds an element of depth as you look through the cutouts in the front layers down into the separated background. There are many ways to provide for this interval, the easiest of which is to mount one layer or layers on the back of a set of artists' stretchers and the others on the front, as was done to achieve the effect in color plate C-25. Think about it a minute and you will realize that either the front or the back set of layers can be mounted on the stretchers before doing the appliqué or embroidery, but not both. Probably it is better to pre-mount the front since it will usually have more layers and all the openings. After both elements are finished and mounted, a network of lacy stitches of one sort or another can be stretched between them if desired, or such stitches can perhaps be worked across the openings.

When the work is completed, the stretchers can be framed. But this method does not allow light to penetrate to the bottom layer from the sides of the piece. You may prefer, therefore, simply to mount only the tops of your front and back panels, if you are making a wall hanging, to a two-by-four or similar board attaching them to its front and back edges and letting the lower portions hang free, a mounting technique used in color plate C-23.

Generally, the bottom layer is not pierced in reverse appliqué, but there is no reason why this has to be so. A logical extension of this idea is to attempt to design double-faced fabric for room dividers or other panels that are to be viewed from front and back.

Mixing techniques rather than keeping each in its own tight compartment is a more satisfactory way to create, and it helps to generate new ideas. Reverse appliqué works well with other kinds of needlework, as the illustrations in this book show. Some other promising combinations are the use of a piece of cloth worked all over in honeycomb smocking for the bottom layer where it will not be cut through, the use of very open cutwork with or without buttonhole bars for a top layer, and the adaptation of faggoting stitches or other openwork seam finishes in some of the top layers.

Fig. 5-15. Yellow lower layer of the two-level stitchery by B. J. Adams shown in color plate C-14. Stitchery, punch needlework, needleweaving and lace stitches. (Courtesy of Norma Papish. Photograph by Clark G. Adams.)

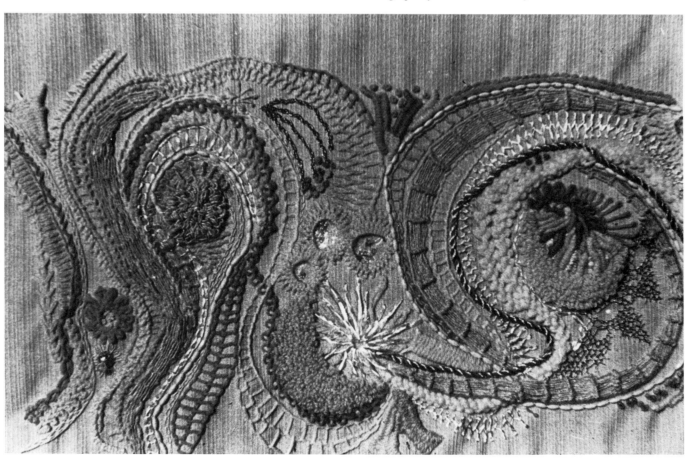

Technical Problems

As you begin to make your reverse appliqué pieces larger, particularly in designing hangings and banners or anything else that is suspended from the top, you may find, even though you were very careful about fabric grain, that you have difficulty keeping the layers flat or in preventing the work from buckling. This is partly a defect inherent in the reverse appliqué itself (but one which can usually be corrected) and partly a lack of understanding of the basic nature of this kind of needlework.

We have seen how reverse appliqué resulted from a misinterpretation of the mola-making process. Until the former was invented, there was no stitchery of any kind, including the mola, that involved laying four to six pieces of cloth one on top of the other, leaving them virtually intact, fastening them together at irregular intervals, and yet expecting the product to lie absolutely flat. In the mola panel, only the bottom layer remains a single piece of cloth. All the upper layers are cut into many sections before they are finally sewn down. This knowledge can help rescue a reverse appliqué hanging in distress. Now it is the top layer that must remain intact, but the lower layers can be slit apart wherever this will not interfere with the design. If advisable, excess fabric in the lower layers can also be trimmed away after this is done. When the elements of the design are very close together, it can be difficult to do this slitting once the hanging is completed, and so, in some cases, it may be easier to use stacks of small patches and baste these behind the areas that will be done in reverse appliqué instead of piling up complete layers. In either of these two cases, it may be necessary to add a lining after the work is completed.

Many people run into trouble because they fail to understand that as soon as you put two or more layers of cloth one on top of the other and anchor them together at intervals, you are, like it or not, in the realm of quilting and you must follow its rules:

Wherever possible, work from the center out. This applies to all basting also. If the layers should slip a bit as you go, they can be trimmed at the edges when you are finished, but the work will be flat and the grain will not be pulled seriously out of line where it matters most, especially after you gain experience.

Tie all the layers together with some kind of stitching at fairly regular intervals over the whole surface of the hanging. This anchoring does not have to be as close as ordinary quilting where you are keeping non-woven batting from shifting and bunching up, nor does it mean that you necessarily have to take all your reverse appliqué stitches through to the bottom layer, which would be tedious and is clearly not always possible anyway. It does mean, however, that any large area of your panel that remains unstitched should be tacked together with a bit of embroidery, trapunto (Italian quilting), or by some other means. Simple tufting may be all that is needed. Thread a needle with a short length of yarn or other heavy thread, sew down through all the layers, and come up again near where you went down. Tie the two ends of the yarn together.

Another thing to watch in both large and small hangings is the bottom layer. If large areas of it are left exposed and it is not somewhat heavier than the layers above, it may be structurally weak and tend to buckle, or it may simply be less opaque and thus unsatisfactory from a visual point of view. Should this be the case, doubling the bottom layer ought to solve the problem. The doubling can sometimes take the form of a lining for the whole panel.

Fig. 5-16. A reverse appliqué sampler in progress. There is little
that is not possible provided the one limitation of leaving a
place to hide the hems is observed.

Notes on Design and Color

Reverse appliqué is not as limited as many people seem to think who confine their patterns to monotonous circles within circles, ovals within ovals, etc. Figure 5-16 shows some of the other things that can be done. In fact, it seems there is little that is not possible provided the one limitation—leaving a place to hide the hems—is observed.

Since the technique is fairly simple, even a beginner can soon give attention to questions of design. Basically, it is a matter of dominance. If you are careful to pick layers of similar cloth in different hues of about the same brightness and intensity for your early trials, you are forced to concentrate on color and you quickly realize that the problem is to make one shade dominate and to see that either warm or cool colors are made more important. How you stack the layers may make it easier or more difficult to do this, but sometimes a hard-to-handle fabric *must* be placed on the bottom, so your ability to switch fabrics around can be limited.

In working with analogous and complementary color schemes, your problem is still one of making something predominate, but you will then be thinking in terms of value and intensity.

When tackling textured fabrics for the first time, simplify the problems involved by eliminating color entirely. Make a collection of white fabrics with pronounced textural differences. You will find they group themselves into yellowish whites or grayish whites. Use only one or the other group so that the element of warm versus cool is removed and you can concentrate on shiny versus dull, etc. Like colors, textures can be compatible or incompatible, and one should dominate the others. It is in working with textured cloth that you are most likely to run into the problem of a difficult fabric that can be used as the bottom layer only.

When making a sampler or wall hanging, see if you can finish the piece in such a way that the technique is emphasized. One way to do this is to cut the top layer the usual length and make each succeeding layer a little longer so that it shows and so that you can see clearly which piece is stacked on which (fig. 5-17). You might then cut the excess vertically, stopping the slashes just below where the design begins (fig. 5-18). Then finish the edges as desired.

Fig. 5-17. In samplers and panels, each layer in reverse appliqué may be left longer than the last to show the technique.

Fig. 5-18. The extra-long section may be slit vertically.

Transparent fabrics are easier to work with than one would imagine since narrow, neat hems are difficult to detect when the work is done. Shadow embroidery (open herringbone stitch or some other lacy-looking stitch that can form curves and be widened or narrowed at will) is very effective when worked on the lower layers and perhaps the top layer as well for contrast.

Fig. 5-19. A reverse appliqué pillow in felt by Lynda Ford Voris. Mrs. Voris finds felt extremely suitable when teaching certain groups, particularly the elderly. (Courtesy of the artist.)

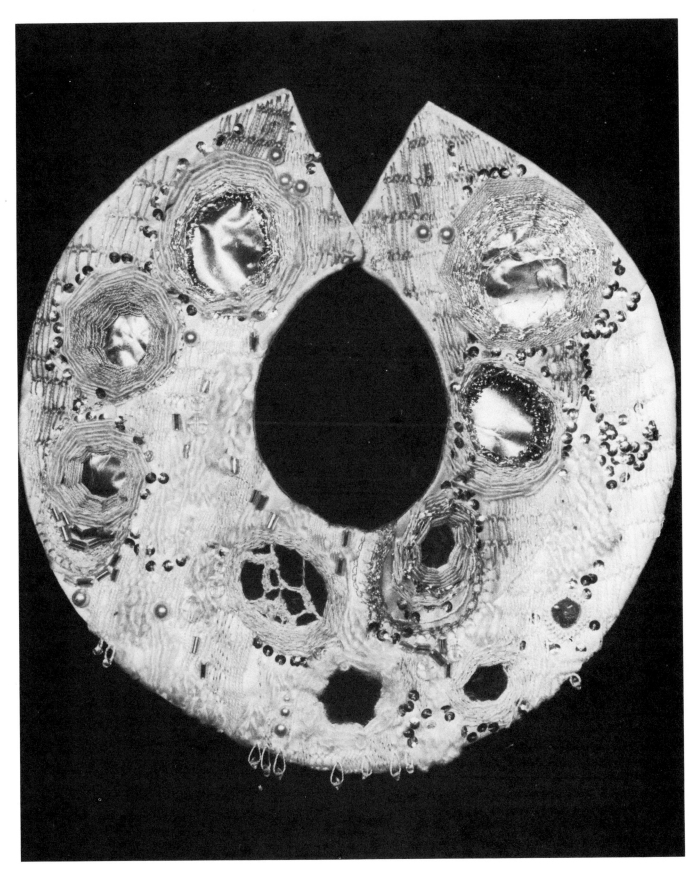

Fig. 5-20. *Lunar Dust*, a collar by B. J. Adams, 4½-inches wide, machine and hand stitching. (Courtesy of the artist. Photograph by Clark G. Adams.)

Fig. 5-21. *Black Blossom*, a stitchery panel by B. J. Adams, machine reverse appliqué and hand stitching. (Courtesy of Mr. & Mrs. Allen A. Kaufmann. Photograph by Clark G. Adams.)

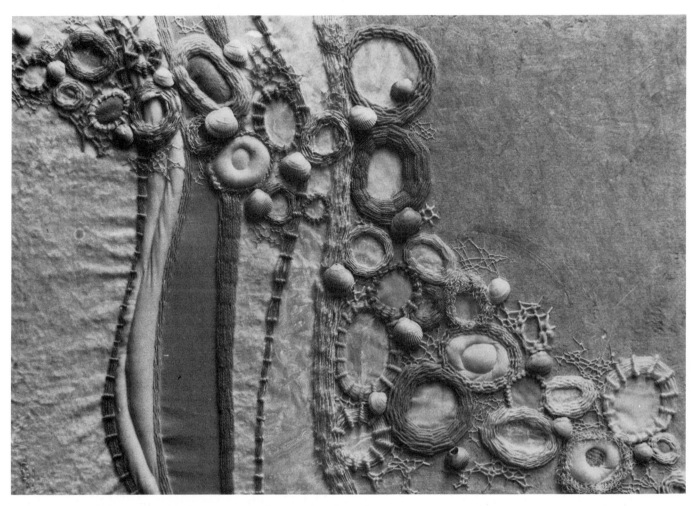

Fig. 5-22. *Surface*, a stitchery panel in whites and grays by B. J. Adams, 35 × 23½-inches. The design is based on surf and sand. (Courtesy of the artist. Photograph by Clark G. Adams.)

6.

Collecting Molas, Making Things, Etc.

The Cuna Indians of San Blas have given us not only the molas themselves but two appliqué techniques as well. We can use all three to decorate our homes, our clothing, and to spark our creativity. It is ironic that a remote and isolated people should have contributed so much to the world from which they have carefully kept themselves apart.

Buying Molas

With the involvement of the United States in Panama and the Canal Zone, it was inevitable that molas should have been brought back to this country over the years as collectors' items. Now that exhibitions of them have toured art galleries all over the nation and high-fashion mola garments have become popular, the demand has burgeoned, and, while anyone who sets out to obtain a genuine mola will probably meet with success, the quality may very well be extremely poor, for the supply of good molas is limited, and people with little talent, or those who take inartistic shortcuts, can now sell their shoddy goods at high prices with little difficulty.

In most parts of the United States, it is easiest to find molas for sale in museum shops, although their selections tend to be limited and, as elsewhere, the quality now varies greatly. Usually you will be shown only unmatched panels; I do not know if you ever see a complete blouse in such a store. Many other gift shops that specialize in imports carry molas, too, as do some large department stores. Sometimes you find the panels advertised in art or craft periodicals. Tell your neighbors and friends that you are interested in buying molas, for they are often sold privately by people who have lived in or visited Panama. Someone in your local weavers' or artists' guild may know of such a source, particularly if you are in a university town or near an air force base where members of the community may have been to Central America or have visited there from time to time.

Long before a passion for worn and faded clothes from past eras became a fad with young people here, mola blouses were worn to a frazzle by Cuna women, then taken apart and the panels sold to eager tourists in Panama City and elsewhere. On occasion, this is objectionable because the work has faded unevenly or in such a way as to make the piece unattractive. Normally, though, fading is hard to detect. On the other hand, there are molas that make striking wall hangings but that were obviously never meant to be worn. These, surely, were made for sale only and cannot be considered in the same category with mola designs that the Indian women make and wear themselves.

How do you choose molas? Whether or not you are prepared to take a trip to Panama, begin by acknowledging the fact that large numbers of them are made directly for foreign purchase rather than home use and that, even if you had access to the latter, you might not be able to recognize the difference without having had the opportunity to examine hundreds of panels and to know the Indians intimately. Nor, with no extensive catalogs available, can the ordinary person recognize the age of the mola he is considering or whether it is a copy of a traditional pattern or an individual's unique creation. Some of the books on molas will give you a little guidance, but not much. What, then, do you look for?

Workmanship is important, of course. No one wants sloppy or inept work. You frequently see molas that are coming apart because the stitching was not close enough or the thread was not pulled all the way through the material. In some, the thread is not suitable for the fabric either in color or thickness, and the cutting may be less than skillful. Curves, for instance, may be flattened out in places instead of flowing gracefully. Watch also for molas that are off-center. This may or may not make a difference depending on what you want to do with them. Many molas, by the way, are not absolutely square. But slightly irregular shape does not detract from an outstanding design.

Shoddy fabrics are also seen frequently in San Blas molas, but here again, blanket judgments cannot be made. Like our patchwork quilts, molas over the years have been made by people who used what cloth they could come by. At one time the coconut boats had a monopoly on the sale of cloth but now the Indians buy from many sources. Often, a piece of poor stuff was incorporated into a mola in such a way that its value was enhanced, and it stands as a tribute to the artistic talents of the worker.

Under workmanship we can include some of the simplifications of the mola technique of the past few years that were adopted in order to meet the inordinate demand for San Blas appliqué. Some of these are merely poor imitations of older types, but others are new and interesting.

It is for its design and visual effects that we rate the mole so highly—the way all four quarters are balanced but never identical, the brilliant colors and the Op art effects they often produce, the graphic motion that is sometimes achieved, and the backgrounds that are often as interesting as the foregrounds. Many people also seem interested in the fresh eye with which the Cuna women view industrial products of our civilization. Assuming that the workmanship is of acceptable quality, it is these things that make the panels so widely sought after, especially in art circles. In buying them, be guided by the advice often given to collectors of painting and sculpture: collect what particularly appeals to you personally. Then, if your purchase does not increase greatly in value over the years, at least you have something you enjoy owning and looking at.

Fig. 6-1. An unusual-looking two-color mola. Here the technique is inlay and the mola-maker must have been thinking in terms of shapes instead of lines. (Courtesy of the Field Museum of Natural History, Chicago, Illinois.)

Wearing Molas

Or enjoy wearing! You can sew a mola to your T-shirt or jacket, a fad that originated among the young people of Panama. Or entertain your guests sporting a complete mola blouse, if you can find one, over a pair of blue jeans. The teenagers in Panama dress that way and decorate the jeans with patches like those in Figure 2-44.

The vogue for women's high-fashion clothing which incorporates molas continues in many circles. They are easy enough for the home dress designer to make, provided she can get the molas she wants in the size she needs, and always much more economical. Naturally, you use the panels whole and do not cut them up. Then, as B. Altman & Company, a New York department store, suggested in an ad for such garments, after you wear them for five years you can frame them!

Because the molas offer so many possibilities, it is impossible to give more than general advice about how to incorporate a mola into a garment. What is possible depends on the size of the mola or molas in hand, your own clothing size, and the styles that you can wear successfully. Basically, the idea is to find a flat area that is large enough for the ornamental piece and will show it to advantage. To begin with, choose or draft patterns for loose, boxy clothes based chiefly on rectangles. There must be no shaped seams or darts, and fullness, if any, should not be located within the area where the mola will be placed. Look for suitable commercial patterns among those designated as particularly easy by the various pattern companies, or find instructions in one of the many books now on the market that shows how to make simple clothes without patterns.

In making tops and jackets, keep the mola below the armhole (see color plate C-19) where it will not have to be cut into. The width of the panel will dictate the length of the blouse, and it is usually more satisfactory to finish the bottom of the garment by binding it rather than to try to hem the mola. Some Indian blouses have velveteen yokes, and these enhance the appliqué panels beautifully. A similar effect can be created by making the classic European peasant blouse (fig. 6-2) out of velveteen. This has slightly-puffed raglan sleeves and is gathered all around the neck with a drawstring. Use a mola panel for the lower front, and, if you have a matched pair, for the lower back also.

A pair of molas can become a pair of sleeves in kimonos or similar garments that have long, wide, straight sleeves. At least 2 inches of the fabric used for the main part of the garment should probably be placed at the ends of the sleeves.

Although molas come in many sizes, the larger ones are harder to obtain, and those who wear size 16 and over may find it difficult to follow the suggestions above satisfactorily. For them, and for people with limited dressmaking skills, aprons may be the best idea. Since these aprons are strictly for dress wear and will never see a kitchen, velveteen and other rich fabrics may form the background for the mola.

One apron is made by attaching the top of the mola to a strip of fabric that will bring it as far down from the waist as desired (fig. 6-3). The two sides and the bottom of the resulting rectangle are then bound and the top gathered to a waistband long enough to be tied in back.

Another apron consists of a long rectangle with a hole to admit the head (fig. 6-4). A mola is attached to the bottom front. It may be seamed to the bottom of the apron, or the apron may be made longer and the mola may be bound across the top and attached to it as a wide, deep pocket. Here, too, a pair of molas may be used, one in front and one in back. To finish the garment, attach ties to front and back just under the arms. A second pair of ties may be placed farther down if desired.

The alternative to using real molas is the adaptation of the mola technique as used by the Peace Corps cooperative. This allows any kind of pattern to be used and any part of a garment to be decorated. Cut a duplicate of the pattern piece that is to carry the decoration. Use

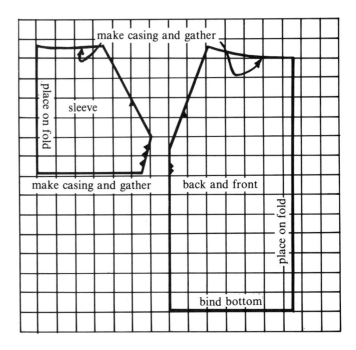

Fig. 6-2. Pattern for classic European peasant blouse, medium size. Enlarge this by transferring to a grid of two-inch squares. Slit front/back and sleeve down the center and spread or overlap to make larger or smaller dress size. If necessary, add fabric to sides of mola the color of the top layer or blouse.

artists' tracing paper or tissue paper for this. Indicate the seam allowance, and do not carry the design, which you will draw on this piece of paper, over into it. Use any desired mola technique or reverse appliqué, but limit the number of layers where too many would be awkward or hinder the draping quality of the garment. Wherever possible, when transferring the design to cloth, do not cut out the main fabric piece entirely, but leave extra seam allowance. This kind of decorative work is not likely to draw up as when doing heavy embroidery in a similar situation, but much handling may cause the edges of the cloth to fray or stretch, and it is better to put the pattern back on when the ornamentation is finished and to do the final cutting to exact size at that point.

Cuna women and girls who live in the part of San Blas where modern clothing is worn often decorate their dresses with small birds or other motifs taken from the mola. These can be placed on the bodice near the shoulder or at intervals around the skirt. Be sure before beginning that the motif you choose is one that will stand on its own when not accompanied by all the other embellishments that surround it in a mola.

Tote bags made from molas are another popular idea (fig. 6-5). Many molas are really too large for this kind of treatment unless an outsize bag is wanted. However, there are many smaller molas that are more suitable, and the larger ones make handsome cylindrical needlework bags (fig. 6-6). Here again it may often prove more practical to make your own decoration to suit the space you want to ornament. Other popular accessory ideas are women's hats and men's ties and sashes.

Fig. 6-3. Apron with mola decoration.

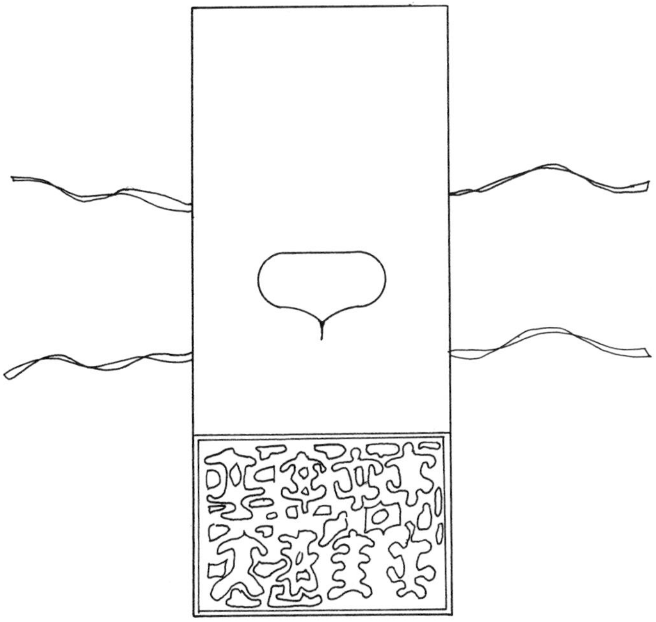

Fig. 6-4. "Sandwich-board" apron with mola decoration.

Fig. 6-5. Tote bag with mola decoration.

Fig. 6-6. Cylindrical needlework bag with mola decoration.

105

Using Molas in Home Decoration

Molas are also used in home decoration. Most people either frame them or turn them into pillows, but they have also been used effectively as place mats or otherwise incorporated into table linens. They might also be used, Oriental fashion, as banners to fill and decorate the tops of open interior doorways (fig. 6-7). They are well suited for this because they hang flat and do not drape. The simplest way to make these is to bind the mola and mount it on a backing fabric large enough to form a sort of cloth frame and with enough extra fabric at the top so that it can be folded over a rod that has been hung across the top of the doorway. These little ornamental hangings, of which there are usually three, should stretch all the way across the doorway opening. For a narrow aperture, one mola may suffice with two narrower harmonizing panels worked in San Blas appliqué and mounted similarly on either side. Your choices will be limited by the size of the doorway and the size of the mola or molas selected.

Fig. 6-7. Japanese doorway ornaments with mola decoration.

San Blas Appliqué and Reverse Appliqué

There is a vast difference between these two processes. The San Blas method is pure appliqué and a way of achieving a line which is multicolored whenever there are three or more layers of cloth. The line may bend around to enclose a shape, which may then be embellished with fillings of various sorts, but when we do this kind of work, we still think primarily in terms of line. In reverse appliqué, on the other hand, we think in terms of shapes.

The San Blas appliqué method, being hitherto unknown except to a few, has not yet made its contribution to contemporary fiber arts. It is a wide-open field for experimentation, and anyone who cares to enter it will have his or her work cut out for him for a long time. Experiments with color alone should yield interesting results. One could also play with monochromatic and analogous schemes, or pastels. Neutrals could take one into the realm of texture, where one would probably get away from the narrow lines preferred by the Cuna women, since many textured fabrics would simply not lend themselves to such treatment. Transparent fabrics are another possibility. Finally, there is the whole field of combined techniques.

Some may also want to work with braid or bias to obtain results similar to San Blas appliqué. A most promising idea is to work within circular rather than rectangular shapes, although much contemporary embroidery employs the circle to the point of monotony. But thinking in terms of a circular or oval framework could bring fresh ideas to the technique of the traditionally rectangular mola.

Reverse appliqué, having been around for a good dozen years, and being very popular, has already been subjected to the kinds of experimentation suggested in the paragraph above. The illustrations in this book were chosen to show reverse appliqué mixed with other techniques such as surface embroidery and quilting. Wall hangings seem to be a favorite in this area, often with separated layers. Surprisingly, there is little soft sculpture to be found, though this form is popular now and reverse appliqué could certainly be adapted to it.

Reverse appliqué also lends itself well to the decoration of clothing, especially in yokes, pockets, collars, cuffs, and other places where extra fabric body may be required, though its use will not guarantee that you can do without interfacing in those places. Avoid multiple-layer reverse appliqué where you want the fabric to drape. The technique is often used for pillows, but it has a special appeal in stuffed toys where its carved surface can supply a variety of textures but cannot be pulled apart by tiny fingers as easily as ordinary appliqué.

Technical Considerations

The work we have been discussing largely results in easy-care products that do not require pampering. Molas are washed regularly by the Cuna women, and you can do the same. As with anything you care about, avoid excessive wringing and twisting. Dry them face down on a kitchen or bathroom counter and, if at any time you feel they need ironing, turn them face down on several thicknesses of towelling and steam them gently, holding the weight of the iron in your hand. This will preserve the carved look. The same advice goes for any San Blas appliqué or reverse appliqué that you make yourself out of washable, dyefast fabrics.

Drycleanable work can be put into a coin-operated machine or sent to the dry cleaners with instructions not to press it. This is good advice for any embroidery. No matter how exellent your professional drycleaner has proved otherwise, cleaners tend to overpress all forms of embroidery.

Soft sculpture and framed wall hangings or those with found objects can be kept clean for a long time simply with gentle vacuuming. If something more drastic is needed, upholstery cleaning techniques are in order. When washable soft sculpture is dunked in the tub, use your hair dryer to get most of the moisture out afterward.

When larger pieces in reverse appliqué pucker a bit, or when banners and wall hangings that are suspended from a rod do not hang perfectly straight, blocking or stretching will usually solve the problem. Most people shy away from this process until they have tried it a couple of times and realize it is not half as difficult as it sounds, especially in the light of the excellent results it gives. Do not expect it to perform miracles, though. If you paid no attention to the grain of your fabric, or otherwise mishandled your materials, blocking may not help at all. Also, fabrics treated with finishes that cause them to snap back to their original shape after washing, steam pressing, etc. cannot be blocked successfully.

To block, use a board that is soft enough to take rustproof pins or tacks without hammering, but hard enough to keep them in place. Some soft woods may qualify, but the best material is fiber insulation board. Your piece should be marked on one side with a one-inch grid, then covered smoothly with clear plastic. This can be attached with a staple gun. The piece to be stretched should not have been hemmed, lined, or otherwise finished. Draw a pencil line all around it ½-inch *outside* the seamline or hemline, where it will not be seen in the finished hanging. Using this and the grid on the wallboard as guides, pin or tack the piece you are stretching to the blocking board. If you are using pins, a thimble will help.

Stretch the panel as much as you can, beginning at the center of one long side and then going directly opposite to the center of the other long side. Proceed next to the centers of the shorter sides. Placing the pins no more than an inch apart, continue to stretch the hanging, alternating long and short sides as before, each time putting the next pin directly opposite. Unfortunately, when you have reached the corners, you may find that the object is not tight enough. Gradually pull two adjacent sides tighter by withdrawing the pins and reinserting them a little farther out.

Bibliography

Area Handbook for Panama, DA Pam 550-46, by Thomas E. Weil et al. [Washington, D.C.]: G[overnment] P[rinting] O[office], 1972. "One of a series of handbooks prepared by Foreign Area Studies of The American University." Background material on Panama to help broaden the all-too-narrow view given in printed materials specifically on the Cuna Indians.

Bothwell, Dorr and Frey, Marlys. *Notan: The Dark-Light Principle of Design.* New York, Van Nostrand Reinhold, 1968. Design problems dealing with negative and positive space. Paperback.

Brown, Lady Richmond. *Unknown Tribes, Uncharted Seas.* New York: Appleton, 1925. A fascinating account of a voyage to San Blas in the days when you sailed your own boat to get there. Most of the author's huge collection of molas and other Cuna artifacts were given to the British Museum, but a few are in The Museum of the American Indian in New York City.

The Butterick Fabric Handbook: A Consumer's Guide to Fabrics for Clothing and Home Furnishings. Irene Cumming Kleeberg, ed. New York: Butterick, 1975. Dictionary form. Introductory chapters give some insight into the manufacturing process and today's fabrics and finishes.

Dean, Beryl. *Creative Appliqué.* London: Studio Vista/New York: Watson-Guptill, 1970. By one of England's most distinguished embroiders. Includes general instructions.

Enthoven, Jacqueline. *The Stitches of Creative Embroidery.* New York: Van Nostrand Reinhold, 1964. An especially clear, attractive presentation of embroidery stitches to combine with appliqué. Surface stitches only. Also in paperback.

Ficarotta, Phyllis. *Sewing without a Pattern*, a Bantam Minibook, FX4556. New York: Bantam, 1969. Only one of many paperback books that show how to make very simple garments, some of which might be used to incorporate molas.

Frew, Hannah. *Three-Dimensional Embroidery.* New York: Van Nostrand Reinhold, 1975. A logical field for experiment with both San Blas appliqué and reverse appliqué.

Gray, Jennifer. *Machine Embroidery: Technique and Design.* [New York]: Van Nostrand Reinhold, 1973. A new edition of a well-known English manual.

Holloman, Regina. "Acculturation and the Cuna." *Bulletin: Field Museum of Natural History*, vol. 40, no. 7, July 1969, cover and pp. 4–9. A good, short account of Cuna life.

Hornung, Clarence Pearson. *Handbook of Designs and Devices, 1836, Geometric Elements Drawn by the Author*, 2d rev. ed. New York: Dover, 1946. An excellent source of ideas for appliqué designs.

Justema, William, and Justema, Doris. *Weaving & Needlecraft Color Course.* New York: Van Nostrand Reinhold, 1971. Specifically for those who work with thread and fabric. Bibliography gives a fairly complete listing of the more conventional basic books on color.

Kapp, Kit S. *Mola Art from the San Blas Islands.* [Cincinnati, Ohio]: K. S. Kapp Publications, 1972. Mola panels from the author's collection, almost all reproduced in black-and-white. Informative captions clarify the subject matter of the designs.

Keeler, Clyde E. *Cuna Indian Art: The Culture and Craft of Panama's San Blas Islanders.* New York: Exposition Press, 1969. A detailed description of Cuna arts and crafts including the mola by a careful and intelligent observer.

———. *Land of the Moon Children: The Primitive San Blas Culture in Flux.* Athens: University of Georgia Press, 1956. One of the better first-hand studies of Cuna life though the author is a geneticist rather than an anthropologist.

Kelly, Joanne M. *Cuna.* South Brunswick [N. J.]: A. S. Barnes, 1966. A picture of Cuna life.

Krøncke, Grete. *Mounting Handicraft: Ideas and Instructions for Assembling and Finishing.* New York: Van Nostrand Reinhold, 1967. How to make pillows, handbags, hangings, etc.

Laury, Jean Ray. *Appliqué Stitchery.* New York: Van Nostrand Reinhold, 1966. How to do appliqué, with an interesting section on color and one on reverse appliqué which the author calls "cut-through work." Also in paperback.

Newman, Thelma R. *Quilting, Patchwork, Appliqué, and Trapunto: Traditional Methods and Original Designs.* New York: Crown, 1974. Instructions for the four techniques with pictures of traditional work from several parts of the globe and a good deal of avant-garde work.

"San Blas 'Appliqué.'" *McCall's Needlework & Crafts*, Fall-Winter 1963-64, pp. 130–1. First use of the term, *reverse appliqué.*

Seitz, William C. *The Responsive Eye.* New York: Museum of Modern Art, 1965. An exhibition catalog whose brief text describes several of the phenomena of Op art.

Short, Eirian. *Embroidery and Fabric Collage.* New York: Scribner's, 1971. Design for needleworkers. Considers general principles, including color, applied decoration, and stitchery as a means of artistic expression.

Stout, D. B. *San Blas Cuna Acculturation: An Introduction*, Viking Fund Publications in Anthropology, edited by Ralph Linton, no. 9. New York: Viking Fund, 1947. Don't let the ponderous title put you off from this interesting and most informative first-hand description of Cuna life. Includes an extensive bibliography of earlier writings on the Indians.

Textile Museum. *Molas: Art of the Cuna Indians . . .* Washington, D.C., 1973. An exhibition catalog with black-and-white illustrations.

Timmins, Alice. *Making Fabric Wall Hangings.* [London]: Batsford/[Newton Centre, Mass.]: Branford, 1970. Filled with ideas for unorthodox approaches to appliqué, and includes an interesting section on designing from cut-paper shapes.

Wassén, S. Henry. "Some Words on the Cuna Indians and Especially Their 'Mola'-Garments." *Revisto do Museu Paulista.* Nova Serie, vol. 15, pp. 326–39. San Paulo [Brazil], 1964. Includes two extremely brief first-hand descriptions of the mola-making process, one of them in Spanish.

Wilson, Erica. *Embroidery Book.* New York: Scribner's, 1973. Classic English embroidery techniques to combine with appliqué: crewel, blackwork, various kinds of whitework, etc. A beautiful book with clear diagrams and instructions.

Index